The
Black
Man-O-logues

A Collection of Stories
Based on "The Black Man-O-logues",
The Stage Play

Created By
Jacquay D. Waller

Written By
Jacquay D. Waller
with Tracy Nicole

Jacquay Waller

The Black Man-O-logues
Copyright © 2013 Jacquay Waller, All rights reserved. No part of this book may be reproduced or retransmitted in any form or by any means without the written permission of the publisher.

A New Day—Publishing

Published by: A New Day Publishing www.anewdaybooks.com
ISBN Number: 978-0-9831695-9-8

The Black Man-O-logues

For my heartbeat, Carys and Asher and my pulse, Courtney ~ I love you all more than you'll ever know.

Jacquay Waller

The Black Man-O-logues

Table of Contents

1. Preface...7
2. Message from the Author..............................9
3. Introduction..13
4. Abused..18
5. Ladies' Man..37
6. The Rapper...54
7. Locked Up..70
8. Unrequited Love...88
9. The Church...106
10. Custody...128
11. Our Wisdom..144
12. True Love...160
13. Afterword...170
14. Aknowledgment..174
15. About the Author..177

Jacquay Waller

Preface

There are enumerable perspectives on black love. There is the love between a husband and wife; the love between a parent and child; the love between siblings; the love between best friends, and the love of a community, etc., etc. What runs through the head of a black man when he is confronted with the subject of Love? "The Black Man-O-logues" offers insight into the question of "How Does a Black Man Express his Love"? In this piece, ten diverse characters offer a montage of experiences and perspectives on black love.

Disclaimer: This is not a misogynistic piece. It is not meant to be degrading or to belittle. The book offers no solutions to various issues it raises. Please, open your mind and be prepared to be transformed.

Message from the Author

I guess you can say that I'm not your ordinary type of guy. Some probably view me as being quite complex, but I prefer to be identified as a "Renaissance man". After all, by trade, I am literally a Rocket Scientist. No joke! My products currently reside on Navy ships. I've always been the creative type. I usually operate outside of the box. In fact, I live outside of the box. My address is nowhere near the box. This is both a blessing and curse at times. Some people seem really appreciative and even envious of the gift to dream and see beyond obstacles. However, there are always those who require more tangible ideas and can't bear to be outside of the box. Did I mention I'm also a Preacher?

Let me provide a brief rundown of my accomplishments, roles and titles: I am a Rocket Scientist, Artist, Actor, Entrepreneur, Filmmaker, Writer, Director, Playwright, an ordained Preacher, an Author, Husband, Father, Son, Brother, and a Friend. I

MESSAGE FROM THE AUTHOR

actually left my job as a Rocket Scientist to attend Seminary. Boy…what a ride! The experiences were like night and day. I was chasing my destiny. How did all of this bring me to this book? I'm glad you asked! While in Seminary, I attended a class called "Sexuality and the Black Church." It was here that the inspiration for "The Black Man-O-Logues" was born. In this class, there were about 35 people – approximately 32 women and 3 men. Men were a huge minority in this course. The few men in the class were expected to answer for the entire male species on all issues pertaining to male/female relationships.

For example, if a female student had an argument with her husband, we took on the responsibility of having to explain his frame of thought. If a colleague wanted to know why men thought sex was so important, you guessed it; we would have to provide the answer. This was just the tip of the iceberg. There were lots of issues, lots of discussions, and lots of arguments. Little did I know that this course would change the direction of my life. What I discovered

The Black Man-O-logues

through this experience was essentially three things: women have many questions about men; men generally don't discuss their emotions; and people say they want to know the truth, but they really don't. I also discovered that the Church (not all churches) generally runs away from the difficult issues because no one has answers. It's a lot easier to pretend the issues don't exist.

My hope is that this book opens your eyes. "The Black Man-O-Logues" is a collection of non-fiction stories wrapped with a layer of fiction. These stories are based on true events. Names have been hidden to protect identities. When audiences experience "Black Man-O-logues", the stage play, some are surprised by the situations presented in the show and the language that is used. You can only imagine some of the responses I've received once these patrons have discovered that the writer behind this material is an ordained minister. Some may even ask why present material in such way that it may disturb, offend, or shock.

MESSAGE FROM THE AUTHOR

Jacquay Waller

MESSAGE FROM THE AUTHOR

As a member of clergy, I grew tired of witnessing many people attend church pretending that everything is okay; pretending to be perfect; pretending lead lives that are free of blemishes; pretending to be the person that they think others want to see. I decided to show the issues as they are without the sugarcoating. This allows all viewers to experience the issues in their fullness and truth. It creates space for real healing to begin. True growth can now take root. God already knows you and knows your issues. God knows the truth and is waiting on you to acknowledge your truth. It's time to be real with yourself.

True potential is achieved when you are open and honest with yourself.

Introduction

The Black Man-O-logues offers an alternative perspective on love. The book examines love in many unexpected ways – many of which women may not want to hear and men may not share due to the fear of being judged. All of these stories are real and based on true events. It is my hope that through exposure, through airing our emotions (since many men are not usually transparent) that we won't be judged, but we will be heard. Unfortunately black men are labeled and enabled by today's media. Any image that radio depicts or television portrays ends up being the gauge by which many black men are viewed. Do we all gang bang? Do we all do drugs? Are we all drug dealers? Do we all dance well? Are all black men athletic? Are we sex fiends? Do we all have "Baby Mamas"? Have we all been to jail? Are we all lazy? Are we all well endowed?

Now, audiences can have the perspective of a black male who cherishes his children and takes his role as a father seriously. There are many people who aren't

INTRODUCTION

aware of situations where men are abused by women. Everyday, there is some man who is getting thrashed by his wife, but no one will ever know. For so long, spousal abuse has only been viewed from one side – the woman's side. Now, let me not be misunderstood. A woman's perspective is very important and I'm not suggesting that we ignore it, but I am suggesting that we also talk about violence towards men in relationships. I would submit that neither is justified and both are equally pertinent.

It is my intention with "the Black Man-O-logues" to use love as a lens to explore various issues that men experience but are often too afraid or too ashamed to confront. This fear and shame may be induced by the thought of being unheard; the fear of appearing effeminate, or becoming the butt of jokes for choosing to express true feelings rather than pretending to be emotionless. It is my hope that with each character presented, readers will explore their own networks or circles of friends and discover those who may be in similar situations. Readers can decide how to dialogue about the issues mentioned and develop a way to bring relief to the situation; even if it is only striking up a good conversation. When more people are discussing these circumstances, the real people behind these stories will have a voice. They will have hope!

This can result in more people being aware of men in abusive relationships; men who truly want to spend time with their kids; men who are true "knights in shining armor". This revelation may allow others insight into the minds of men who are placed on high pedestals, but share our common human struggles. Men who are transparent, open, and honest, but ignored will have a chance to be heard. Men who are products of their environments and unaware of the harm they emit during their plight for success may be enlightened. The men who hide their true identity because society is not ready or willing to accept them without judgment may now be able to be true to themselves and others. Men who unselfishly give to their families, communities, or to strangers with the

INTRODUCTION

hope of it being paid forward may be able to experience a sense of appreciation and gratitude. This could prove to be a welcomed acknowledgement to the men who shatter the façade of love portrayed through media with the understanding that love is a process.

After all, love requires work and commitment. Love is not perfect and Love needs time. Love is like a garden that displays various colors and aromas. Gardens can provide fruits, vegetables, herbs, beautiful scenery a peaceful refuge and more. One element that all gardens have in common is that they ALL need WATER. All relationships need LOVE. It appears in many colors, flavors, shapes and aromas. Moreover, love provides the sustenance for relationships to grow.

The Black Man-O-logues

Jacquay Waller

The Abused

What do people imagine when a boy gets "beat up" by a girl? How about when a man is beat up by a woman? Abuse is far too often viewed as solely physical. Emotional and mental abuse can be just as damaging. This is the first of many stories that are never, ever told...

"What did you say to me punk ol' ass nigga?" Shae tossed her head to the side swinging her long black hair behind her shoulder after cutting in front of a couple standing in line. She displayed an intimidating air of confidence smoothing out her tight spandex royal blue mini dress that exposed every curve her body possessed.

"I said the line is back there!" The big guy yelled pointing to the back of the line.

Shae acted as if she heard nothing and continued placing her order for her drink. "Yeah, lemme get a Petrone Margarita?" She spoke loudly so the bartender could hear her over the music. The couple standing behind her didn't appreciate Shae rudely stepping in front of them and ordering a drink without so much as an excuse me or even a glance in their direction.

Careful not to spill her drink, Shae turned around and directed her attention to the big stocky dude with the build of a former football player standing next to a small petite woman. Clearly his size didn't scare her. "Who in the hell do you think you talkin' to?" Shae got closer to the man invading his personal space. She yelled over the loud music still blasting in the club. "You betta back the fuck up!" Shae waved her free hand in the guy's face.

"Look lady, be easy. My lady and I are just trying to enjoy ourselves tonight. All this ain't even necessary." The big guy held his hands up in the air and backed down.

"Just what I thought. Yo punk ass ain't gon' do shit! Fuck you and yo lady!" Shae looked them both up and down, then took a long swig of her drink. Then she bobbed her head to the music. "Damn! This a good ass drink!"

Darnell pushed his way through the crowded dark club in an attempt to get to the bar after spotting his wife rolling her neck in the midst of talking to a big guy. He couldn't make out what was being said over the loud music but knew it was bad. He knew somehow his wife had started some shit again because she always has something to say. Darnell arrived just in time to witness Shae toss the remainder of her drink on the guy and his lady.

"Keep talkin' to me like you crazy. My husband will whoop yo ass for talkin' to me like that. You better get the fuck out of my face! Now I need another drink fuckin' wit yo ass! My drank was good as hell too!" Shae waved her hand in both of their faces. The petite victim of Shae's actions looked at the big guy in disbelief. "Yeah, you better get yo man. He don't know who he fuckin' wit'," Shae continued. They both looked shocked, appalled at her behavior and the words that were coming out of her mouth. They were equally as shocked to see that she actually had a man when Darnell stepped up coming to the rescue.

Darnell quickly grabbed Shae around the waist and began pulling her away from the bar to remove her from the club as quick as possible. "Damn girl, I can't take you nowhere!" This wasn't the first time Shae started some shit with people and then threw him out there to defend her just to see if he was man enough to handle it. He turned back to the couple clearly embarrassed and said, "I'm sorry!" and handed the guy a $100 dollar bill. "This should take care of the dry cleaning. I'm really sorry for all this." Darnell didn't wait for a response and pulled Shae out of the club.

"Let me go! I can't believe you gonna just let that nigga disrespect me like that! Ain't you supposed to be my man?" Shae yelled.

"Shae you are drunk! Now stop pulling away from me. Come on now girl! We are going home."

"I ain't ready to go home! Now let me go! Take yo fuckin' hands off me. I need to go back in here and find me a real man. I ain't leavin' wit yo sorry ass. Now get yo hands off me." Shae slurred pulling away from him and adjusted her tight fitting dress and attempted to walk back the other way.

Darnell used all the strength he had to grab her and pull her away from the entrance of the club to prevent any further embarrassment. "Come on and get your ass in the car!"

Shae stumbled as Darnell forcefully pulled her across the parking lot. She fell to the ground and scraped her knee.

"Baby, you okay?" Darnell softened and reached down to help her up.

Shae pushed his hands away. "Don't baby me! Get yo' fuckin' hands off me. Ol' punk ass, weak ass nigga! You couldn't even take up for me in there. You just let that nigga talk to me all crazy. You ain't got no balls! No backbone! Fuck it! I guess I shouldn't expect any more from a nigga like you. You ain't no real man!" Shae laughed and started walking back toward the club.

"Shae come on and get in the car now!" Darnell reached for her arm again. Shae scratched him across the face and pushed him hard in the chest. Shae was still stumbling in her heels trying to maintain her balance. Darnell was fuming now and rushed toward her, ignoring the stares from the people in the parking lot.

"Oh, now you want to be a man? What? You wanna hit me now? Come on! Hit me! Show me you're a man!" Shae taunted him.

"Shae get in the car now!" Darnell grabbed her and pulled her to the car.

"Weak ass nigga! I'm the nigga in this relationship! You hear me?" Shae yelled waving her hands in the air. She was too drunk to fight Darnell and swung at nothing but air. All of a sudden the heel on right her shoe broke.

"Look at what you did! You done broke my fuckin' shoe." Shae reached down and took off the other shoe and held up the patent leather royal blue stiletto with the four-inch heel pointed in the air. "I'm gonna beat yo' ass!" Shae began chasing after Darnell holding the shoe in the air.

"Shae stop! You're making a fool of yourself. Running after me with those cheap ass shoes." Darnell dashed around the other side of the car. Shae was too slow to catch him.

"You ain't gon' be calling me a fool when I beat yo' ass with this shoe!!" Shae was determined to catch him. "Cheap? Cheap! My shoes ain't cheap nigga. Oh, and you gonna buy me another pair of shoes. No, yo ass is buyin' me two pair of shoes. You think I'm playin' wit yo ass! Stop runnin' from me ole' punk ass nigga!" Shae was panting trying to catch her breath, forced to slow down.

All the alcohol she drank had finally set in. Darnell seized the moment by grabbing her and putting her inside the car. Shae had collapsed in his arms. Darnell gritted his teeth ignoring the comments from the onlookers in the parking lot. He closed the door after securing her in the passenger seat. Then he paused to take a deep breath and walked around the car and climbed into the driver's seat of his black on black A8 Audi. Shae was slouched in her seat with her head propped against the window and mouth wide open. Fortunately she was passed out. Darnell sat staring at her bad weave hanging from her head and began to focus in on her disheveled appearance. His eyes traveled down her body to her scraped knee and on down to one bare foot and one shoe without a heel. The chipped polish on her toenails was where his glance ended. He then shook his head in disgust.

What happened to my wife? She wasn't like this when I met her. She was loving, polite, caring, and just plain nice. Now this heffa ain't nothing but a Hellraiser and a mess. I should have paid more attention to all the things she told me about from her childhood about how her mother and father would beat up on each other before her father left her life for good. I guess when people grow up seeing drama in relationships, like an abusive parent, that becomes their idea of what normal is. Even though the relationship felt good, it just didn't feel normal to her, I guess. She's always looking for something to fight about. I get up in the morning and I'm brushing my teeth too loud. If I take my clothes off I'm junking up the house. If I don't shave I'm looking like a homeless, broke ass nigga. We never have enough money but she can't take her lazy ass to work. Nothing is ever good enough for her. I can't even think of a time when she's not complaining or trying to fight. She just has too much damn mouth! Always embarrassing me in public. I don't know how much more of this shit I can take! How much can any man with anything swinging between his legs take from a woman like her?

Darnell put the car in gear and drove off.

The following week Darnell was on his way home. He had his shades on and the sunroof back listening to the sounds of Kirk Franklin. *"Oh, oh, oh … you look so much better when you smile …"* Darnell bobbed his head to the beat. Getting through the bumper-to-bumper traffic seamed a little worse than normal today. Darnell turned up the music and decided to just enjoy the ride home as much as he could. Then thoughts of Shae entered his head.

The words she yelled at him time and time again began to ring in his ear. *"You weak ass nigga! I need me a real man! Why you can't clean up this damn house? Why you dress like that? You so damn lame! How I end up with a sorry ass nigga like you anyway? Nigga you can't do shit for me! Ole' pussy ass nigga!"* Darnell couldn't help but feel helpless as his thoughts took over and drowned the music out in the car.

I feel like a loser. I was always taught to live right. I was taught to take care of women and treat them with respect. I would never lay a hand on my mother, my sisters or any woman for that matter. My parents didn't raise me like that. I just figured if I did everything by the book that everything would line up perfectly. I got a beautiful home, a job I love, and a crazy ass wife! I wake up to her naggin', cussin', bitchin', and hittin' me. "Darnell why you didn't push the toothpaste from the bottom of the tube? Darnell fold the end of the toilet tissue when you finish. I want to grab a folded end of the tissue. What? You should've did what I said and I wouldn't have had to knock yo' ass upside the head. Darnell why you chew your food like that? Stop actin' all perfect and shit! Darnell, what the fuck I gotta do around here to get you to clean up? I know it's my shit. If you see it, you need to pick it up. What, you gonna leave me now? Well go ahead. Everybody else in my life left. You ain't no exception." I go to bed with her naggin', cussin', bitchin', and punchin' me… "Darnell why you wear that shit to bed? You so damn lame! Oh, you tired from working all day? Nigga be a man! I don't even feel like I'm sleepin' with a man. You shouldn't have been in my way and you wouldn't have got scratched. You so damn weak! I can't believe you still here, puttin' up with my shit."

"Honk! Honk!" The person driving the car behind Darnell was growing impatient. Darnell had unconsciously eased his foot off the gas slightly slowing down as the power of his thoughts made him less eager to get home. Then it hit him like a ton of bricks. He suddenly realized he didn't want to live like this anymore and some things were going to have to change in this situation. The only problem was he had no idea how to deal with Shae.

After arriving home Darnell was greeted by Shae at the door.

"Hey baby!" Darnell forced a smile placing his briefcase on the floor by the door.

"Don't hey baby me! What took you so damn long to get here? I been here all day by myself." Shae rolled her eyes.

"Baby, now you know I was at work. Come here. Stop all that fussin' and give me some lovin'!" Darnell took his jacket off and placed it on the back of the chair. He walked toward her and attempted to put his arms around her waist. Suddenly, his head was thrown to the side after feeling the sting of Shae slapping him hard across the face.

"You got off a fuckin' hour ago! You mean to tell me it took you an hour to bring yo' ass home? And go hang yo' damn jacket up! You ain't got no maid round here!" Shae yelled.

"Come on, Shae! Do we have to go through this shit everyday? I'm tired of this mess! You know there's a lot of traffic in this city. I may work twenty miles away, but it takes me an hour to get home in the evenings. Why are we even having this conversation again? I'm sure you're going to bring it up again tomorrow. You should be tired of this shit! Now can we just let it go and make up?" Darnell asked in another effort to diffuse the situation. This only made Shae angrier.

"Oh you real funny with yo' punk ass! I ought to crack yo' nuts right now for talkin' crazy to me! You know I'll do it too!" Shae stood with both hands on her hips looking Darnell directly in the eyes.

"Baby, just calm down. It's cool." Darnell calmly pleaded.

"It's cool? It's cool? What's cool? You shole' ain't! Damn! How did I end up wit' a weak ass nigga like you, anyway?" Shae raised her voice walking around Darnell, looking him up and down, as he stood there listening helplessly. "You dress like a nerd. You talk like this." Shae teased speaking in a proper tone. "And you a punk! How in the hell you just let me talk crazy to you like I do. Nigga you let me treat you any ole' kinda way!" Shae smirked and turned toward Darnell. "Wait, where is our money? Didn't you get paid today?"

Darnell ignored her and walked to the refrigerator to get some water. He insisted on keeping the situation under control. "So how was your day today, baby?"

"Oh, you still talkin' to me? Why?"

Darnell looked back at her and shook his head. His patience were growing thin.

"Nigga, why you lookin' at me? I'll knock the shit outta yo' ass!"

"Come on baby, what's for dinner?" Darnell tried his best to disregard her crazy behavior.

Shae walked away still talking loud. "I can't believe this negro just asked me about dinner. Nigga ask yo' mama! She like you more than I do anyway? Why am I still here? You gonna' come home one day and I'm gonna' have my new man here waitin'. Then you'll see what a real man looks like. You see a real man wouldn't take no shit like this. He woulda' been done knocked the taste outta my mouth and dared me to say somethin' else." Shae walked around the room putting on a show for herself. She noticed Darnell wasn't paying her the attention she wanted him to and turned around to walk back toward him.

"What, you gonna leave now? You gonna leave like everybody else in my life did. Well go ahead. I don't need yo' sorry ass anyway. I need a real man that don't take no shit. That's the kinda nigga I'm lookin' for. An ole' rough neck. A nigga that got more than a traffic ticket on his record! I need a man who'll talk crazy to me when I need it and then turn around and make me feel like a woman." She put her arms around herself and moved her hands down between her legs and walked closer to Darnell. "See he would take me in his arms and fuck the shit outta me. He'll just wreck it! Have me callin' his name all kinda ways until I lose my voice. That's what I need. I don't need some ole' negro who gonna' open doors, ask me what I need, ask me what I want, ask me if I got mine … you know what I'm sayin'? Nigga, I'm from the hood. I need a hood nigga!" Shae pushed him hard in the side of his head with the palm of her hand.

"Shae I'm warning you. Stop puttin' your damn hands on me. Now I love you and we can work this out, but this ain't the way."

Shae laughed and mimicked him. "Stop putting your damn hands on me! Wit yo proper ass. You ain't gonna' do nothin'. See Boss, Crime, and Tony ain't havin' dat from they women. They'll give 'em the business in a heartbeat. But you ... you know what you do ... Nothin'! Not a damn thang! You just work and come home. You so ... innocent. You know what ... I got a good mind to call Alexis, Aleze, and Chanel so they can come over here and beat that ass. Since they men ain't havin' it, I'll tell 'em that mine is a push over and he ain't gonna' do nothin'. You know what you gonna' say? I don't hit women! I don't hit women!" Shae taunted him and pushed him in the side of the head again. This time she pushed harder than the first time.

"Shae I'm telling you. Don't put your hands on me again." Darnell gritted his teeth and restrained himself from reacting physically. He knew that her harsh remarks came from a place of pain all these years he had tried his best to love her past her pain to no avail.

"Or what? Nigga you ain't gonna' do shit! Stop interruptin' me! Now, what was I sayin'? Oh yeah, we probably just gonna' take our time and take turns beatin' that ass. Now what? Say somethin'! That's what I thought. I'm goin' shoppin' nigga!" Shae laughed and pushed him in the side of the head again. She reached for her purse off the counter and began to walk away.

Darnell shook his head and pulled his arm back and balled up his fist and yelled, "I told you not to touch me again!" Darnell punched her in the face and knocked her the fuck out…

Jacquay Waller

The Ladies' Man

There are some people who've tried love and it failed them. There are some who've tried love, and they betrayed it. Then, there are those who love to experience love in its many colors, shapes, and sizes. And of course there are those who cherish love best, in its physical and emotional state. Is there a wrong way to love?

THE LADIES MAN

The sun was rising as Fleetwood stood at the door of his townhome kissing his date goodbye. He gave her one last firm grip on her butt before sending her on her way.

"God knew what he was doin' when he made you girl. You know you my baby, right?"

His date giggled.

"I'll talk to yo' sexy ass later. Let me know you made it home safely." Fleetwood said watching her from behind in her tight mauve-colored mini dress and five inch heels as she walked to her car.

Fleetwood tightened his robe and bent over to pick up the paper before walking back inside. He walked into the kitchen and poured himself a cup of coffee. His place was decorated so nicely, it looked like it could be a model home. The beige and brown colors with a hint of teal green kept it masculine looking. Everything was modern and high tech from the fire place to all the flat screens. If it didn't have a remote, it had a button to push. It was a dream bachelor pad. The place was kept immaculate due to the housekeeper he hired to come in twice a week to cook and clean. Fleetwood was living a life that only some dreamed of.

Ring … Ring.

"Hello."

"Oh, good morning baby."

"Yeah, I just got up. I'm about to drink my coffee and read my paper."

"You missin me more and more, huh? Well, I'll have to see what I can do about that." Fleetwood smirked.

"Thank you baby, I hope you have a great day too."

"No, not goodbye. We don't say goodbye. I'll talk to you later."

"Right, that's better."

"Alright baby. Yeah." Fleetwood hung up his cell phone and gently dropped it in the pocket of his robe.

After fixing his coffee up with milk and sugar Fleetwood walked out onto his balcony. He paused at the to door and took a deep breath of the fresh outdoor

THE LADIES MAN

air. He then sat down putting his feet up on the patio table to enjoy his coffee and read the paper.

"What's up Fleetwood man? I see you had you another hottie last night. I think you have a different woman there every night. I'm just over here with my dog Rusty living vicariously through you. I think you might just be the 21st century Mac!"

Fleetwood was momentarily caught off guard and looked up to see his neighbor sitting on his own balcony, which was connected to the right side of Fleetwood's balcony.

"What up Fleetwood?" His neighbor called out louder and proceeded to stand up from his lounge chair wearing a wife beater with boxer shorts and tube socks half covered by a plaid robe.

"Joe." Fleetwood raised his cup of coffee in the air and nodded.

Joe was his neighbor and could be annoying sometimes but Fleetwood didn't mind talking to him. He could tell Joe looked up to him and thought he could teach him a little something.

"So, what's the word Fleetwood?"

"Hey, I guess I can say women love me just as much as I love them." Fleetwood flexed.

"All I can say is, you know how to pull some hoes."

"Now see, I don't refer to women as bitches and hoes, and things like that. I treat them like the special beings that they are. I thank God for women, especially my black women.

"I hear ya but black women can be a handful sometimes. I had to venture away from my sisters a little bit. They just got too much mouth for me." Joe shook his head.

"Now see, that's where you wrong." Fleetwood sat his coffee on the table in front of his chair and adjusted his robe. "Ya see, a black woman will love ya, they'll feed ya, they'll care for ya ... they'll cus' ya, they'll fight ya, and they might even nag ya a lil' bit, but they're special. They are nurturers and want to make sure the man that they love is well taken care of. I just hate to see them hurt." Fleetwood shook his head.

THE LADIES MAN

"Oh hell naw!! I wouldn't have the patience or desire to deal with a hurt woman."

"Sometimes they are the best kind because they need you to help them feel better about themselves and it don't take too much. I just speak to 'em when I get a chance. I ask 'em how their day is going ... I tell 'em they look nice ... I compliment them on their looks and attire ... I smile at 'em, I flirt with 'em, I show them attention ... In public and in private. I make sure they feel important. Women want to know they are a priority."

"That's all fine and good but I saw a young lady coming out of your place just last week and she was a little on the heavy side." Joe laughed. "You sure don't discriminate do you?"

"It's two things I don't do ... I don't playahate and I don't discriminate. I could care less what religion or ethnicity they are. I don't care if they're fat, tall, short, skinny, dark, light, heavy, thin ... whateva. I just love me some women and as for their age ... it ain't nothing but a number."

Ring…Ring…Ring

Fleetwood reached into the pocket of his robe and pulled out his cell phone. He answered the phone and held one finger in the air to his neighbor telling him to hold up a minute.

"Hey baby."

"I miss you too. I was just thinking about you."

"Now you know I want to see you. I just been really busy that's all."

"I know we were supposed to go to the movies. You just tell me what day you want to go and I'll make it happen. I'm sorry baby. You should know you been on my mind."

"Of course I'll make it up to you. Even if it takes me all night to do it."

"Yeah, I want to see you in that little lace number that I like."

"Girl, you gone make me come through this phone and get you."

"Alright, baby."

"Talk to you later."

Fleetwood hung up his phone and slipped it back into his robe pocket. He took a sip of his now luke warm coffee. "Now where was I?" He leaned back and relaxed.

"You were just telling me what a pimp you are." Joe laughed after hanging on to every word of Fleetwood's phone conversation.

"Hey, I take that as a compliment. I can't help it if I got game! Fleetwood popped the collar to his robe. "Naw seriously man, I'm not a pimp."

"You could've fooled me. I mean, look at you. You don't even have to work. You just chill all day and do whatever you want on your ladies' dime." Joe said leaning on the rail of the balcony. "Now tell me that ain't pimpin'!"

"Well, look at it this way. I don't hang out on no track. I ain't got no hoes! And I don't make women sleep 'round with people for money and then bring it back to me. That's a pimp right?"

"I mean yeah, if you're speaking literally."

"Well, it seems to me that a lot of pimps are educated in the streetz, but I don't know many that are educated in organized institutions besides those that are surrounded by barbed wire and metal and provide you with three hots and a cot." Fleetwood explained.

"What does that have to do with you and your situation?" his neighbor looked confused.

"What I'm sayin' is, I'm educated. I went to a historically black college and graduated with honors. Right after school, a major pharmaceutical company even hired me. I make, or at least I used to make a good living on my own."

"Well, explain to me how you came to have so many women then, Mr. Educated Man."

"I used to do spoken word at this little after hours spot while I was in college. That was when I realized I had the power to make women happy on a whole 'nother level. I was able to touch them without laying a hand on them. I just love seeing the ladies happy and being responsible for turning their frowns

THE LADIES MAN

upside down. I remember when I first got my groove. I used to start my show by saying Where are my beautiful ladies? They would just grin and laugh. Then I would say Madam, Madomoiselle, Je t'adore! Je t'adore! Dat's a lil' French for ya'll that ain't traveled much! I would tell 'em Ya'll ain't ready! Ya'll ain't ready! The women would just go wild hanging onto my every word. Some would throw panties on the stage and one time, I even got some handcuffs!"

His neighbor laughed holding his stomach. "Man, I bet you had them women willin' to do anything for you! I wish I coulda been a fly on the wall at one of them shows. You probably got them Sugamammas huh, you know the ones that want to take care of their man?"

"Actually, I have had my share of Sugamammas, but I show them all the love and respect they can handle. I'm always up front with them. I always tell them, 'I love making love to you, but I'm not ready to settle down … if we go there … and you look like you want to go there, I know I do … there are no strings attached … we are just friends with benefits … can you handle that?'"

"Damn, I need to write that down. That sounded good! You mean to tell me that shit works?"

"It's the truth. Women respect honesty and there are a lot of sisters out there that need attention and need to be saved. Ya see, so many dudes are married, dating white women, or dating each other, I have to make sure there's enough of me to go around."

"What, you got a service going on? How much you chargin'? Wait, you sure you don't need someone to fill in every now and then? Cause if you do, then I'm your man."

"You got it all wrong. I don't charge a fee, cause that would make me a hoe, right?"

"Well, if the shoe fits. I know you gettin' more than you tellin' me outta this. Shit, I could use a few extra dollars myself. Man you don't even go to work!" Joe dramatically stated thowing his hands in the air.

"Many women do give me money. They take me shopping. They buy me things. They cook for me. I've even had a few to bathe me down and wash me up. I didn't ask for any of these things though. They just do them for me. I mean I work. I do have a job. I have a real important job."

Ring…Ring…Ring

"Wait, let me get this." Fleetwood struggled to pull the cell phone out of his robe pocket. He looked at the caller ID and answered.

"Sheryl baby. Where you been?"

"I know. I've been waiting on your call."

"I know how busy you are."

"I thought you forgot about me. How long you gonna make me wait?"

"I don't know if I can wait that long. You got me going through withdrawal over here girl."

"Okay. Have a safe trip back. Call me as soon as you land. I got something for you and you better be ready."

"Oh really?"

"Girl, don't tease me like that."

"You better take you a nap on that plane."

"Alright baby."

"Talk to you later." Fleetwood ended the call and placed the phone back inside his robe pocket.

Joe stared wide-eyed enamored by his phone conversation. "Who are all these women and where do you find them and how can I be down? You think I'm playin'?"

Fleetwood laughed. "Well, many of these women are professionals, like doctors, teachers, lawyers, engineers, scientists, realtors, and the list goes on."

"How in the hell do you juggle that many women? Sista's at that! Nigga, school me!"

"Wait now, I don't sleep with all of these women, many of them, but not all of them. And I always protect myself, and them. I also get tested every six months. Sometimes these women just want a little bit of attention. They want to be noticed; to be loved; to be touched. Sometimes, we just lay butt-ass naked in the bed together, under flickering candlelight, sharing some of our dreams, goals, and maybe even a little poetry. Hell! Sometimes we even talk about God."

"Damn man, it seems like you've got it down to a proven science. Got me over here wanting to write all this shit down. You need to write a book about this shit. Hell, I'll buy it!"

"Look, I just want women to know that all brothas out there ain't bad. There are still some brothas that know how to treat a woman. Some of us still love women. Some of us still love black women. Ya feel me?"

"Yeah, I hear ya, but I don't know how many women would like you juggling them like you do. I don't think they would be too happy with you tellin' so many women the same lines, especially using the 'L' word. You just take it to a whole nother level. I would hate to see you get caught up in a situation. I think it could get real ugly and these days it could even get you killed. These bitches out here crazy nowadays. They'll cut yo dick off and mail it back to you."

Fleetwood laughed and shook his head. "Man, you are crazy! I've never been involved in any kind of situation like that. Now, I know I ain't quite right... but somebody gotta step up and let these Nubian queens know that they're beautiful and they're appreciated and they're important. Let's get some things straight. I don't use the 'L' word. That's not in my vocabulary. That word suggests a permanent connection. I also don't say good-bye. I say talk to you later because good-byes are forever."

"Man, where are you gettin' this stuff from." Joe chuckled. "I just think you've got to have a cap on how many women you have, right?"

"No, I wish I could be with all of them at once. I wish I could marry them all and give them all the respect, the love, and attention they need. But I know I can't do that."

"Damn, right. Whew! You scared me. I was beginning to think you had lost it for a minute."

"Well, it's my dream and my fairytale to please women."

"I'm just sayin' how do you keep it from becoming a whole lotta drama? I'm just sayin', you can get cut playin' the wrong woman."

THE LADIES MAN

"Because I'm always straight up from the beginning. I don't mislead any woman. I just say you can love it or hate it. They know what they are getting into from jump and they don't mind at all. In fact they get everything they want and sometimes more out of the situation. I'm dedicated to the women in my life. If no other man on this earth wants to love my sistas and give them their props and attention; I will. You betta believe that shit!" Fleetwood picked his paper back up, leaned back and turned the page.

The Black Man-O-logues

Jacquay Waller

The Rapper

In a day and time where what's on the outside is much more important than what's on the inside and where what you feel and what you say are disconnected, ignorance flourishes. Unfortunately, it's attractive to many. How long will it last? When does self-love, love of neighbor, and acknowledgement of familial struggle step forward to take its rightful place?

Camelot stood in the mirror admiring his iced out grill. Two girls walked slowly across the set putting an extra twist in each step. Camelot could see them looking at him in the reflection of his mirror. He turned around and the first thing he noticed was bare ass peaking out from under the back of their dresses.

"Hey Camelot!" the girls sang out simultaneously causing a mischievous grin to creep across Camelot's face.

Camelot grinned and threw his head up in response. The girls giggled and kept walking by.

"Hey wait, you in the red. Come here." Camelot ordered unable to take his eyes off of her body.

The girl in the red complied and turned around walking up to Camelot.

"Damn baby! You sexy as hell." Camelot looked her up and down.

The girl covered her grin with her hand and mumbled, "Thank you."

Camelot pulled her close and ran his hand down her back suddenly grabbing the bare part of her butt. The girl gently pushed him away.

"Stop. Don't do that."

"Come on gul, don't act like you don't like it."

"I'm serious. Don't handle me like that." The girl got loud, rolled her eyes and walked away pulling her dress down.

"Oh, you one of those ol' uppity bitches who think she better than everybody. You ain't better than no other ho on this set. Bitch this my video! Actin' like somebody owe you somethin'." Camelot grabbed between his legs. "Trick, I don't owe you nothin'!"

Camelot's manager rushed over when he saw the girl storming off. "Camelot, man come on! You'll have plenty of time to mess with these girls after the video shoot. Now, we are paying by the hour." His manager explained.

Camelot laughed and cocked his head to the side. "You act like it's comin' outta yo' pocket. It's always all work and no play for you. Just chill out man. I can't stand bitches like that. They just blow up if you touch 'em a certain way. They don't want you huggin' 'em, kissin' 'em, grabbin dey ass, or nothin'. And if you do, yo' ass might catch a charge. Even if you get too close to 'em you might hear from dem red dawgs cause dey shole be datin' 'em."

"Camelot can you at least wait until the end of the shoot to start messing with these girls? We need them for the next shot." His manager was getting frustrated. Unfortunately, he was used to this behavior from Camelot and knew he was wasting his breath.

"Fuck dem bitches! I don't need them! They need me! I hate workin' wit hos like dat. A lot of 'em on they way out anyway. They don't even want to wear the stuff I like … and they in my motherfuckin' video! They don't understand that less is more. Shit, I know what sells. Tits and Azz! That's what my niggas want to see. That's what make yo' video hot which make folk buy yo records and get you mo' spins."

"You are absolutely right Camelot. Come on, let's get this next scene shot okay."

"Aight. That's cool." Camelot went back to admiring his reflection in the mirror.

"You know these hos be up on a nigga! They love my grill and they get wet wit my ice. You just don't know--" Camelot smiled at himself in the mirror bobbing his head to the beat of the loud music coming from the set.

"Will you come on? I don't want to hear anything else about these girls." Camelot's manager interrupted him again appearing irritated.

Camelot playfully grabbed him around the neck. "Man, I said chill wit all that. You wouldn't even believe me if I told you some of the things that me and deez guls don' done. I'm talking 'bout forget about fantasizing about two guls at once. Have you tried five at once? Umm, Umm, Um!"

"Not one of these hoes is worth losing what I got at home, much less five. I had my share of fun over the years. This shit is still new to you. Just wait, it'll get old." The manager explained as the two of them walked back on set.

"Pussy will never get old!" Camelot looked at him like he was crazy.

"Whatever." His manager shook his head. "Let's go do the last shot of this scene so we can send these extras home and we can break for lunch. You have an interview during your lunch too. Come on. Let's go. Time is money."

Camelot and his manager walked onto the set and the music got louder. The director of the video took over directing Camelot and some of the girls in the shot. As Camelot's manager walked away he overheard noise coming from outside of the building where the video shoot was being shot. He walked outside and was greeted by a crowd of protestors holding up signs, chanting and stomping on Camelot CD's. The signs read "Don't buy trash!", "Stop degrading women!", "We must stop Camelot!".

Camelot's manager ignored the crowd and dashed back inside locking the door behind him. He rushed over to the director and whispered in his ear. The director yelled, "Cut! Let's break for lunch."

"Hold up! Wait, we didn't finish the shot. I was in my groove. I'm lovin' the ass hangin' out of the dresses. That shit is hot!" Camelot held his pants up in front with one hand as he slowly walked off the set.

"Camelot come walk over here with us. We need to talk to you in private." His manager motioned for him to follow them. The three of them walked into the next room and the director closed the door behind them.

"What's goin' on Mane? I don't have time for no bullshit." Camelot asked.

"Look, there are some people outside protesting. You know the ones that are not too happy with your music." His manager explained.

"And what? Fuck 'em." Camelot nonchalantly replied and threw one hand in the air.

"Look, they could cause trouble that we don't need. We could do all of this work in vein if they prevent the song and the video from being released. I just want us to play our cards right, that's all." His manager explained.

"Mane, they tried to do that shit with my boy's song "Tip Drill". Hoes talkin' bout how … how … what's the word? How … degraded the song is and shit. But it's true! And sexy as hell. A credit card sliding down a gul's ass ? Ooh … nigga! That was the shit! You know how popular that song was in the clubz? Dat's money Baby! I got's to get mine! I ain't got time to be listening to deez bitches and weak azz niggas cry about my music." Camelot preached overdoing it with hand gestures.

"Camelot, I hear you. I just need to have something to say to these people so the situation doesn't get out of hand."

"Tell 'em don't buy it! Tell 'em don't listen to it! Tell 'em if they don't buy it, somebody else will. I'm just giving the people what dey want to see and hear." Camelot justified.

"Hello." Camelot's manager answered his phone looking directly at Camelot as he took the call. "Yes, you can come in. I'll have him ready for a quick interview. Sorry about the mess outside." His manager hung up the phone looking at Camelot to make sure he had read between the lines. "Hey, I'm going to get the guy that's doing the interview for you. I need you to be on your best behavior. I'll be right back." His manager stepped out.

"Best behavior. I ain't no fuckin' child! What you see is what you get right here! Can't I get mine? Can I come up? I ain't hurtin' nobody? I ain't out in the streetz killin'. I ain't never spent a night in jail." Camelot continued where he left off. "And I don't do harmful drugs. Dis is how it's done! I ain't the only one doin' it! See how many records a nigga sell if he don't do it like this dis. Tell 'em before they try to judge me, I got kids! I got a sister, a mama and a grandmamma too. And they all love me. They all proud of me. Dis is what I do to take care of dem. I'm just a brotha tryin' to be progressive. They don't know me. Where is my iced out OBAMA chain? I be gettin' political and shit! Mane, what you think about all dis?" Camelot asked directing his question to the video director who stood there listening in silence the entire time. He was amused by Camelot's antics.

"Well, honestly I think any type of publicity is good publicity. I also think those people outside are going to promote your music better than you can alone and probably triple your sales." The video director and Camelot slap hands.

"Playa! Now that's what I'm talkin' bout! You need to school my manager over there." Camelot pointed to his manger, who was walking toward him with a guy in a suit following close behind. "I'm feelin' real American Gangsta right about now." Camelot folded his arms and posed with his head cocked to the side. "King Kong ain't got nothin' on me!" Camelot yelled and threw both hands in the air. The video director chuckled and shook his head. "Man, wasn't that line in *Training Day*?"

"Huh?" Camelot looked confused.

"Nevermind." The video director raised his eyebrows shaking his head with a grin.

Camelot's manager walked in and interrupted the conversation. "Camelot this is Jake. He is from Kontraband Magazine out of LA. He would like to conduct a quick interview with you before we finish up the shoot."

Jake stepped closer to Camelot and shook his hand with a firm grip. "Nice to meet you."

"Yeah, what's good?" Camelot responded. "Where you from, Compton?"

"Um, no actually I'm from San Diego."

"Actually… I was just jokin' mane. Loosen up. You got your suit and tie on and shit!" Camelot laughed punching him in the arm. Jake forced a laugh as they both sat down and took out his recorder.

"Um, do you mind if I just record this for the story?"

"Dat's cool."

"Okay, Camelot. So what is your real name?"

"Nigga, my name Camelot and dat's as real as it gets."

"Okay. How do you feel about the comments you hear saying that you are selfish and everything you do is all about you and you have no respect for our sisters?"

"I show love for my people by helpin' bring dem up. Now, I ain't perfect but I ain't all bad either. I love my sisters. That's why I always give them first dibs in my videos." Camelot laughed.

Jake shook his head. "You have kids right?"

"Yeah."

"Would you ever let your kids listen to your music and how do you feel about other kids listening to your music?"

"Hell naw. I don't let my kids listen to my music cause it ain't made for them. It's made for adults. If other folks let they kids buy and listen to my music, who am I to tell them, No? I say Thanks! Preciate ya!" Camelot laughed.

"Um, okay. So where would you say you got your work ethic from?"

"I got it from my Mama. I saw my Moms struggle when I was comin' up, and I made a promise to myself that I gotta do betta. I never want to struggle if I don't have to."

"What would be your response if someone asked you if you talked to your mother with the language used in your music?"

"Nigga, what the fuck kind of question is that? I'll punch anybody in the mouth for askin me somethin' like dat." Camelot looked furious.

"Um, calm down okay. I never said you talked to your mother that way."

"Don't tell me to calm down. Look mane, Just keep my mama name out yo mouth. I would never talk to my mama that way. She would beat my ass! Even now! I respect my elders! Well, at least I try to. I mean I'm a good person."

"I'm sure you are." Jake responded sarcastically.

"Mane this interview is over!" Camelot jumped up and stormed off. His manager ran after him.

"Camelot, what's up?" His manager asked grabbing him by the arm to stop him.

"Man, I don't like that nigga. He seemed like he was tryin' to talk down to me. Like he betta than me or somethin'. Now I did the stupid interview. Can we go finish shootin' my video." Camelot grabbed the front of his pants and began walking toward the set again. "Cause I'm tryin' to come up. It's my turn; My time to shine. I ain't bout to be out here strugglin' like these other niggas."

"Look Camelot, I know your heart is in the right place. Let's just go finish this video." His manager stated.

"Damn right my heart is in the right place. I look out for my people more than anyone I know. I show love for my people. I give these sistas their five minutes of fame and sometimes they get a little somethin' afterwards. Now you can't tell me they don't appreciate that shit. Just ask them. How many people can say they make dreams come true? Answer that question." Camelot threw his hands up and walked

THE RAPPER

back onto the set and smacked one of the girls on the butt. "Alright now, let's get it! Where my director at? It's time to make some dreams come true!

The Black Man-O-logues

Jacquay Waller

Locked Up

Here is another fad in the black community…being locked up. It's cool when one can pretend to be hard, while living a life surrounded by shrubbery, stoned walkways, and golden knives and forks, because it's all make believe. It doesn't count! Most times what happens behind bars stays behind bars. Who's available to comfort one's hidden ailments? What does it take for someone being stared down by love to stare back?

"Number 8-4-5-2-1-3 you have a visitor." The prison guard yelled as he unlocked and pulled back the door of Crutch's cell. Crutch was startled and jumped when the cell door slammed open.

"Come on, move it! Let's go! You don't have all day." The prison guard yelled.

Crutch slowly got up off of his bed. Then stood up and adjusted his bright orange overalls before the guard walked in to handcuff him. Then he followed the guard out of the cell and down the corridor passing by the other jail cells.

"Where you think you goin' nigga?" An inmate yelled.

"I'm waitin' for ya when ya get back!" Another inmate yelled.

A musty odor with a mix of bleach filled the air. Crutch kept walking and appeared to be impervious to the comments. His eyes stayed glued to the back of the officer's head in front of him. His face remained expressionless upon entering the visitation area.

LOCKED UP

"Alright Crutchfield! You don't have all day." The guard announced allowing Crutchfield to pass by. He walked over and sat directly across from his visitor remaining expressionless.

"Hey Baby!" Niecie screeched, excited to see her man.

Crutchfield looked down at his handcuffs and nodded at Niecie. "What it do?"

Niecie's excitement slowly faded. "Okay. It's good to see you, too." There was an uncomfortable silence until Niecie decided not to waste anymore time. "Look at you! You all big n' stuff." Niecie glanced him over from head to toe. "Don't look like you missin' no meals. You lookin' good Crutch!"

"Hm!" Crutchfield mumbled under his breath.

Niecie's face displayed a serious look now. "I miss you, baby! It's so lonely not having you around. The bed just feels so empty without you. Dawn misses you, and so does Star. They're really having a hard time not having you around. But don't worry. We'll be okay until you get home." Niecie gave a half smile and twirled the end of her hair.

Crutchfield just stared at Niecie in silence giving her a deadly look.

"Well, yo' Ma and Pops say hello. Your brother Daniel said he was puttin' somethin' on yo' books this week and Chip say –…"

"Aight! Aight! I get it!" Crutchfield interrupted. "Tell 'em I said … wait, did you just say Chip?"

"Yeah Baby. Chip said he gon' be up here soon to see bout ya." Niecie offered an approving smile.

"Fuck that Nigga, Chip!" Crutchfield barked.

"Baby, don't worry 'bout him. I'm here to see you right now! So tell me how you doin'?"

"Dat Nigga's the reason I'm in here now!" Crutch yelled.

"Crutch, don't worry about Chip. I shoulda never mentioned him. He don't even matter right now. I'm here with you now. How are you makin' it?" Niecie sounded sincere.

LOCKED UP

"I'm makin' it! A Nigga survivin', damn!" Crutchfield snapped back.

"What's with the attitude Crutch? I've come all the way down here to see about you! To tell you how much you're missed. To tell you how empty and cold the house is without you. How things just ain't the same. How I miss how you would warm up my side of the bed and keep me warm and safe during the night. How just the thought of being with you right now makes me tingle between my legs. I came to tell you how much I love you and I'm gon' be here when you get out!"

Crutch laughed and nodded his head.

"What's so damn funny?" Niecie grew angry in an instant and abruptly caught herself before she snapped. "You know what? Let's just start over, cause somehow we got off on the wrong foot." Niecie adjusted her shirt exposing cleavage from her double D breasts and pushed her hair back with both hands. A grin crept across her face. "Hey Baby! It's really good to see you! I miss you so much! I love you so much! How much longer is it going to be?"

"What? Don't ask me no dumb shit like that. I got ten years in this bitch and I ain't done but six months."

"It's going to fly by and I can't wait to get you back home!" Niecie giggled as she trailed his body with her eyes.

"Ey Shawty. You need to pump yo' brakes!" Crutchfield announced.

"What?" Niecie looked confused.

"Stop wastin' my time!"

Niecie's mouth dropped open.

"You been dippin', huh?" Crutch asked nonchalantly. You kissin' dat pipe? Naw, I know wha it is, You cuttin' that Nigga Chip, ain't ya?"

"Crutch, what are you talking about? I don't even see Chip. I haven't seen him since he dropped off that package to me and the girls. He said you sent it! Look, I didn't come all the way down here for this shit!" Niecie rolled her eyes and folded her arms.

LOCKED UP

"Is that your final answer?" Crutch asked as if they were in the third round of 'Who Wants to Be a Millionaire?

"Naw Nigga! I told you I ain't messin' with Chip! Where is all this comin' from?"

Crutchfield stared right through her in silence.

Niecie clears her throat. "Um, well?"

"Nigga, you don't have no idea of how hard it is in this place! I'm in the place day to day. I'm always lookin' over my shoulder and shit!" Crutchfield looks down and shakes head. "It's fuckin' crazy in here!"

Niecie softened, seeing the pain in his face from his words. "Baby, I'm so sorry you got to deal with all of this mess. Hang in there. Okay? You can do it. You strong. Just stay on your knees. God will see you through."

"Um Hmm …" Crutchfield looked at her and nodded his head.

"And since we're on the subject of knees, you want to know what the word is on the street?"

"What you talkin' bout?" Crutchfield's heart began to pound through his chest and his palms began to sweat.

"Oh, you don't know?" Niecie cocked her head to the side enjoying her position. "Do you want to know?"

"Damn Niecie! Just say it!" Crutchfield shouted.

"Crutchfield, your time is up!" The prison guard yelled walking toward Crutchfield.

"Hold up!" Crutch responded as the guard grabbed him under his arm. "Man, hold up! Niecie just say the shit! What you talkin' bout?"

"I said times up! Now come on." The prison guard forcefully pulled Crutch to his feet. Crutch kept his eyes glued to Niecie as he was being pulled away by the prison guard.

Niecie looked him dead in the eyes and said, "The streetz screamin' you fuckin' niggas in here! Is that true?"

Crutchfield tried to resist the pull the prison guard had on his arm.

LOCKED UP

"Let's go Crutchfield!" The prison guard yelled and pulled harder breaking his resistance.

"Hell naw! Nigga, hell naw! Who said that? Niecie, do you really think I would be laid up wit another Nigga?" Crutchfield shouted still in motion moving in the opposite direction.

Niecie hesitated and then shouted back, "No, but if you were, would you tell me?"

The prison guard pulled Crutch through the door before he could respond. Moments later he was back in his cell.

"Lock down! Close the cells! Lights out! Shut-up! Or else it's a week in the hole!" The prison guard yelled just as everything went pitch black.

Crutchfield sat on the edge of his bed in the same position for hours trying to control the anger that was building inside of him.

The next morning Crutchfield was woken up by the sound of his cell door opening and greeted by the same musty smell. He was getting a roommate and instantly had to wrap his head around sharing the tiny cell. Crutch thought this could probably be a good thing since now he would have some company.

"What up man? I'm Crutch." Crutchfield said as the grungy, overweight cellmate walked in and looked around.

"Oh, what up? Rod." The cellmate cautiously responded.

"That's you up top, but you can sit on my bed if you want. Shit, we got to get used to each other." Crutch grinned.

"Naw, man I'm good. I'll just stand for right now. I mean I know it'll be lights out pretty soon. At least that was what I was told." Rod nervously responded and leaned up against the cell wall unsure of Crutch's intentions.

"I just been in here by myself for a few weeks. It feels like the walls are closin' in and you start to hear your own thoughts." Crutch explained scratching his head while scanning the room. "Man, I don't deserve this shit!"

LOCKED UP

"Yeah, I can believe that." Rod laughed and loosened up. "So what you in for?"

"Man, I was just trying to survive and provide for my lady and my lil' girl. Who don't push a lil' wood and white gul every now and then?" Crutch explained.

"I feel ya'." Rod responded shifting his weight to his other leg. "So, how long they give you?"

"Ten fuckin' years! Man, this the longest I ever been locked up. This shit ain't no joke. In the past it's just been a slap on the wrist, but this some real shit. On the outside it's all cool bein' a D-boy and a Trap Star. Man, I was like a superstar! I always had stacks on stacks, all the hoes I wanted and shit like that! But mane, when you get up in here in this hell hole, don't nothing matter! A nigga just tryin' to survive! Arrrgh! I miss my girl!" Crutch remained seated on the edge of his bed rocking back and forth.

"It can't be that bad." Rod looked for some reassurance.

"Shit, it's worse!" Crutch pulled some pictures out of his pocket. "See, I keep this picture of my gul and my lil' princess with me all the time. I don't go nowhere without this picture. Nowhere! They the ones that keep me from losin' it. They all I got! This stuff up in here, it ain't real. It can't be real. All a nigga trying to do is survive. Shit, if I can just make it to five, I can try to get parole."

LOCKED UP

"You sound like you scared or somethin'." Rod chuckled.

"Nigga, I am scared! Just wait, you gonna see exactly what I'm talkin' about. This yo' first week too!" Crutch shook his head. "You should be scared yourself."

Rod laughed. "Man, I ain't got nothin' to be scared of."

"Shut-up!!" Someone yelled from another cell.

"Who said that? Is that you Cleo? Shut yo ass up!" Crutchfield yelled back.

"Man, these niggas in here talk so much shit behind bars." Crutchfield said to Rod, shaking his head.

"So, what you scared of?" Rod asked.

"I'm just sayin' niggas up in here make it hard. They make it real hard." Crutch's explanation was becoming more intense. "Niggas sweat ya if you too nice of a guy. They don't really care if you believe in God and all that. Niggas just trying to get off up in here. It's so much freakin' goin' on up in here it may as well be Boys Gone Wild! Big ol' niggas hugged up with big ol' niggas. Lil' niggas hugged up with Big ol' niggas. Niggas having sex in the cells, in the courtyard, and always in the shower. And they ain't usin' no protection!"

Rod's grin faded and became a serious one. "Man, what the fuck you talkin' bout? That sound like some gay shit."

"Now don't get it twisted. All of these dudes don't want to have sex. Most of them are made to have sex. If you don't give it up … they take it, or they try to kill ya'.

"Oh, hell naw. I ain't down for no fuck shit like that!" Rod stood tall.

"Look, I'm just tellin' you cause didn't nobody warn me. My last cellmate tried me my second night in here."

"Man, fuck that shit. What you mean tried you?" Rod was clearly disturbed.

"I had to get in that ass and let him know I ain't no punk!" Crutch continued.

"Man, that's what I'm sayin'. I damn sho ain't no punk. So, what happened." Rod's eyes grew wide.

Crutch put his head down. "Shit, they still got me though."

"What you mean? Oh, hell naw!" Rod yelled.

"They got me and it wasn't no escaping."

Rod looked confused.

"Look, there's this group of dudes called the 'Sweethearts'. They ganged up on me when I was in the shower and they knocked me out. Hell, when I woke up, I was in the clinic and I couldn't stand."

"What the fuck? Man, they not gettin' me! I know that! That's some real gay shit!" The cellmate shook his head and paced the floor back and forth.

"These niggas that's takin' it don't think they gay. They say they just imagine it's they girl that's on the outside and just be in the moment. They figure the shit that go on in here don't count, so they just adapt. The niggas that's givin' it up, they gay! At least that's what they say."

"Man, fuck that! All them niggas gay. I don't care what you say. So what you do after that? I know you got them niggas back!"

"For the next three months I spent most of everyday runnin', hidin', and fightin' off them niggas. I kept saying to myself *I ain't gon' be nobody's bitch!* Them niggas was not gonna rape me again. I'll be dead before I let somebody rape me again. These niggas can give it up to all these other niggas if they want to… I ain't givin' it!"

"Man that's fucked up!" The cellmate looked horrified.

"Fuck you, nigga!!" Someone yelled from another cell.

"I know that's you Cleo! You real tough locked up! Just wait til' tomorrow. You gon' be my bitch, nigga!!" Crutchfield yelled back, then returned to his conversation with his cellmate.

"Look, I'm just tryin' to survive in here. I don't want my ol' lady to find out about that shit. I love dat girl and she ain't got to know what goes on here in dis place. Cause when I get out, we gettin' married and gon' add to our family. I was out there in them streets, cheatin' on her all the time, lying about lookin' for a job and workin', chasin' that fast money, them fast women, and them fast cars…" Crutch's voice trailed off.

"Not no mo'! Once I get out of here, I'm a changed man. I'm gonna tell her I love her everyday. I'm gon' show her how much I love her everyday. I'm tellin' you. I'm gon' go to church, get a job, and just do better. But until then, I got to do what I got to do."

"I feel ya man. That's some real fucked up shit!" Rod shook his head.

Crutch stood up. "Listen man, just stick with me and you won't have nothin' to worry about." Crutch stated slowly inching toward Rod.

"I appreciate that." Rod responded and headed toward his bunk.

Crutch grabbed Rod's arm as he walked by catching him off guard. "I said I ain't givin' it. I'm takin' it!" Crutch's grip overpowered him. "Now bend yo' ass over!"

The Black Man-O-logues

Jacquay Waller

Unrequited Love

Marriage is hard work. It is not for the weak hearted. If the truth is told, the white picket fence in marriage ceases to consistently exist. It falls someplace between white and black. Every marriage has its issues. If each side always agrees and never has a differing opinion, it's a lie. That is unless each side is married to itself. Is love truly everlasting?

Purvis walked into the office wearing a black suit and headed straight for his desk. The office was freezing cold as usual. Some employees even kept small space heaters underneath their desks.

"Hey, Purvis!" Mike called from his cubicle.

Purvis stopped dead in his tracks. "What's up, Mike?"

"Hey man, I wanted to ask you what you thought about the new project—"

"What are you doing?" Purvis interrupted staring at Mike's computer screen. "Wait a minute. Those look like female profiles for online dating. Are you –"

"Yeah, man. It's hard out here for a pimp. Man, I'm ready to settle down. What you know about this online dating thang?"

"I know a little more than you think. That's how I met Tisah."

"What!?" Mike was shocked.

"Damn, man. Keep it down. I don't want the entire office to hear." Purvis looked around the office to see if anyone was listening.

"What's the big deal?"

"Look, I don't want everyone in my business. Just be careful. I don't think that online dating thing is all it's cracked up to be."

"What do you mean?" Mike asked.

"I mean my experience is just not turning out quite how I expected that's all. Look, I can't talk now. Let's just meet for lunch."

"Cool, cause I got some questions." Mike couldn't wait to talk to Purvis at lunchtime. He wanted to know what Purvis could possibly mean by online dating not being all it's cracked up to be. He continued surfing through the profiles.

At lunchtime, Mike and Purvis went down to the cafeteria. It was full of people, many conversations, and plenty of noise. They both got their trays and patiently traveled through the food line. There was a station for each type of food. Mike and Purvis made their way to the seafood line.

"Yeah, let me get the baked Tilapia." Mike requested from a heavyset black woman with short black hair covered by a thin net.

Mike collected the rest of his food, got something to drink and checked out first. He walked over to the very back of the room where no one else was sitting. After sitting down, Mike spotted Purvis and waved for him to come over. Purvis complied and headed straight for his table.

"What's up man?" Purvis said sitting down across from Mike.

"Man, this fish is off the chain!" Mike announced with a mouth full of food.

"I'm talking about what questions you have for me?"

"Oh yeah! Man, I just can't believe you used an online dating service."

"Yeah, well me either." Purvis shook his head filling his fork with salad.

"What made you decide to use an online dating service?"

"Honestly, my life didn't quite turn out the way that I had planned."

"At least you met your wife. I mean we all want to meet our soul mate one day."

"That's the thing. I had already met my soul mate." Purvis spoke in a solemn tone.

Mike looked confused. "What do you mean?"

"I mean I had already met the love of my life and I lost her."

"Now I'm all confused. So your wife, Tisah, is not the love of your life?"

"Hell no!" Purvis blurted out.

Mike looked shocked and was at a loss for words.

"Look, it was like this. Me and my girl Shauntel dated all through high school. We were the epitome of high school sweet hearts. I liked her parents and of course they liked me too. She liked my parents and they liked her too. Our parents even liked each other. It was perfect! Man, she was perfect. We were each other's first. I thought it would last forever. I'd like to think she did too."

"So what happened?" Mike leaned in and was all ears.

"Right before graduation, we'd finally decided where we were going to college. She wanted to study medicine and I wanted to study law. Schools from opposite sides of the country made offers of full scholarships to each of us. It was at that moment I had to make the most difficult decision in my life, or at least at that time. Me and Shauntel severed our relationship."

"Aw man, that's terrible." Mike commented holding his drink in his hand.

"It was a mutual decision. It ended on a happy, but bittersweet note. We really loved each other. We loved each other too much to restrict the other from enjoying life ... especially during our college years. Thank you Jesus!" Purvis laughed and threw both hands up at the same time.

"Sounds like it was a good decision." Mike said.

"I thought it was. We each prayed that God would bring us back together for that perfect union after she'd finished Medical School and I finished Law School. It never happened. During my first year of Law School, I was home for a visit when I ran into her, and her husband, and their newborn baby girl, in the mall."

"Damn! I know that was crazy." Mike blurted out before taking another bite of fish.

"Yeah, I was crushed. I felt like such a fool for believing she would wait on me and that we would be together forever." Purvis shook his head.

"So that's why you tried the online dating thing? You had trouble meeting someone new?" Mike asked.

"No, I met a lot of women either at the club or at church. It seemed like all they wanted to do was either go to the club or go to church. I needed some balance in my life. I like clubbin' sometimes and then sometimes I just want to spend a nice evening inside, sipping wine, listening to some Jazz, Jill Scott, or Jodeci and then, you know how the night's gonna end!"

Mike and Purvis laughed.

Purvis continued explaining. "I mean, don't get me wrong, I love the Lord too! I love my church! I love going to church! Just not all the time! Not all day! Not all day Sunday, all night Wednesday, all night Friday, and all day Saturday too? Sorry!"

"Hey, I have to side with you there. I consider myself a spiritual person. I just don't think you have to go to church to show that you love and serve the Lord. I don't think you have to give all your money to the church to go to heaven. That's just how I feel." Mike clarified.

"Well, I pay my tithes, from the gross, not the net! Just give me some balance, that's all I ask! I sometimes wonder if God gets tired of seeing certain folks at church."

"What you mean?" Mike asked.

"You know people who go to church all the time. He probably be saying Ooh Child, weren't you just here? You need a life!"

"Man, you crazy!" Mike laughed.

UNREQUITED LOVE

"Anyway, that's when I gave online dating a try. Well, this is the way I looked at it. I know I ain't no loser. I know I'm a "Looker". I got a lot going for myself. I had just finished law school; I had a great job, a hot ride, and smooth crib in the heart of downtown. I just needed someone to share it with. After all, the years weren't getting smaller. They were growing! And they're still growing. My boy Steve over in Finance recommended that I try an online dating service."

"You talking about Steve that wears the bowties?" Mike rubbed his chin in confusion. "White Steve!"

"Yeah! White Steve! That's him! He was really convincing because he told me that was where he'd met his wife, Pavar."

"I could see that being convincing." Mike nodded taking a sip of his drink.

"Man, I was pumped to give it a try. Why not?"

"Shoot that's how I feel. So what happened then?" Mike grinned real hard.

"Then I met someone very special. Actually she was so special, she's now my wife. My wife of two years and three months to be exact! Umm...Hmmm!"

"Sounds good to me." Mike shook his head and grinned.

"Yep, me too! We connected instantly. She was family oriented and so was I. She was career-oriented and guess what ... me too! She loved the Lord, Hallelujah! She wanted to balance, church, work, and fun. Perfect! She was perfect, or at least I thought."

"Sounds pretty perfect to me. I mean, it doesn't sound like it could get any better than that." Mike said.

"You're right. I mean she's beautiful, and sometimes fun to be around, but our relationship seems to be going in reverse after three years of marriage. We still try to be civil towards each other, be we argue more now, than ever. Things have gotten really boring! In and out of the bedroom!"

"Damn!" Mike's eyes grew wide.

"We used to make love at least twice a week. Now we're good if we get it twice a month. I gotta have it more than that. Please! She used to dress up in sexy lingerie and we would go at it like rabbits! But lately, she seems to be distancing herself from me."

"Man that sounds bad." Mike looked down at his food disappointed.

"Yeah man, it is bad. I mean we argue like regular folks but we don't kiss and make up like we used to. I don't know what changed."

"Are ya'll trying to make it work?" Mike sounded hopeful.

"Yeah, I try to stay fit. I buy her nice things. I talk dirty to her. I don't know what else to do?"

"You think there's someone else in the picture?" Mike questioned.

"I really don't think she's cheating or having an affair. We still go places together and have our good times. But she's treating me more like her friend than her husband. She shies away when I put my arm around her. And when I hug her, she keeps it brief but friendly. Our kisses are no longer deep and wet, but dry and shallow. And the sex ... I think its sympathy sex. Shortly after, she runs into the bathroom and showers, demanding her own space."

"So, what are you going to do?" Mike raised his eyebrows.

"I really want to make this thing work, but she recently confessed she wants out. Her reason … I'm too nice. I'm too much of a goodie, goodie. I'm too chivalrous. Too much of a gentleman." Purvis continued imitating her in a whiny voice. "She said she needs a rough neck. She wants a man who is gonna take charge. She wants somebody who can 'beat it up'. Somebody who can run her head into the headboard and come back with a soft, innocent kiss."

"Okay, now that sounds crazy!" Mike commented.

"That heffa's confused! She don't know what she wants. And I don't think I can give her what she thinks she needs. I would try just about anything, but I don't want to lose myself trying to become someone else. I'm at the end of my rope at this point. I'm just tired of trying to make it work by myself." Purvis let out a sigh and grew quiet.

Mike was at a loss for words and simply shook his head.

After a few minutes Purvis gathered his tray and stood up. "Come on let's get back to the office."

Mike jumped up and followed behind Purvis to dump his tray. "I know it's a little early to ask this but would you ever try online dating again?"

"Hell yeah, but if this thing with Tisah doesn't get any better, I'm through with black women!"

"What?" Mike jumped like somebody hit him. The two stood at the elevator awaiting its arrival.

"Yeah, I said it! From here on out, it's white women, Asian women, and ooh Hispanic women. Aye Mommi!"

"Man, you are too funny! I'm heading back to my desk now to look at some more profiles. I'm going to find my wife." Mike announced and jumped off the elevator and sped down the hall leaving Purvis behind. Purvis shook his head and slowly walked back to his office. The rest of the day flew by and before he knew it, it was time to go home. Purvis gathered his things and walked out of his office to head home.

Purvis beat Tisah home and sat down on the couch and turned on the television. He started thinking about how nice it would be if things with Tisah could go back the way that they used to. He thought it wouldn't hurt to give it one more try to connect with Tisah. The door slammed shut snapping Purvis out of his daydream. Tisah was standing at the counter sorting through the mail when Purvis came up behind her and put his arms around her. Tisah was about to walk away.

"Where are you going?" Purvis playfully asked.

"Whatcha mean, where I'm going? I just got off work too! I'm headed to the shower. I stink! It's hot outside!" Tisah pulled away from him.

"Girl, you don't stink! You ain't even sweatin'! But I can make you sweat!" Purvis teased trying to grab her again.

"Naw, you can go get us something to eat. I need some steam!" Tisah replied avoiding his arms.

"You want some company? We haven't taken a shower together in about a year. You know how I put it down in the shower, don't cha?" Purvis chuckled and began humping the air.

"Yeah, I know. I just want to be alone right now. I just got to unwind." Tisah explained.

"Do you want me to give you a massage?" Purvis asked.

Tisah didn't answer and walked toward their bedroom. Purvis followed behind her hoping to have his way.

"Long day, huh?" Purvis remarked.

"Yep! As usual. Carmen wants me to go on extended travel over the next couple of weeks. I'm supposed to leave Sunday night, but I don't want to go." Tisah rolled her eyes and began to take her work clothes off.

"Awww. That's sweet! You don't want to leave your hubby!" Purvis laughed.

"Yeah, but I got to go if I want to keep my job." Tisah never looked up at Purvis.

"Tisah, are you still attracted to me? Do you know it's been two months since we've made love?" Purvis was serious.

"Purvis, why don't we talk about this later? I really need to shower. I just got home from work and I want to relax." Tisah brushed him off.

"Tisah, we're going to talk about this right now! You've been pushing me off for far too long and I got to know. What's up, Tisah? What's up? Why are you pushing away from me? What did I do? I'm sorry! Can I fix it? What can I do?" Purvis pleaded.

"Purvis, I don't want to talk about this right now." Tisah walked into the bathroom and turned the shower on.

"No, we gon' talk about this!" Purvis yelled and walked in the bathroom and turned the shower off.

"Purvis!" Tisah was shocked.

"Don't Purvis me!" Purvis imitated her.

"Are you certain you want to go there?" Tisah calmly asked.

"Yep! I'm certain!" Purvis shouted.

"Hmph! Okay! Purvis I'm not in love with you! I haven't been in love with you for most of our marriage. A lot of times you get so close to me that it's creepy. It makes my flesh crawl. I think the only reason I married you was probably because you were trying to live right and live your life for the Lord. Don't get me wrong. You're a good guy. I like you as a person. I would love to have you as a friend. I'm just not in love with you anymore. I love you, but I'm not in love with you. Now there, that's what you wanted. Is that what you wanted to hear? You want to hear more? You want to hear that I fake orgasms with you? Do you want to hear that I dream about men I work with and men I see at church? Do you really want to hear that I think you're just too nice of a guy?"

"Naw, I think I heard enough. I'm done." Purvis walked in the bathroom and turned back on the shower

The Black Man-O-logues

and walked back into the bedroom. He turned and looked Tisah dead in the eyes and said, "You were right, you do stink." Purvis left Tisah looking dumbfounded and walked out the door.

UNREQUITED

LOVE

Jacquay Waller

The Church

Men and women of the cloth have very stressful jobs. Once they introduce themselves to the world under the microscope of "Reverend", they are forever haunted by the paparazzi. They are now larger than life and are supposed to be immune from injury and mistakes. Underneath all of the titles, robes, and accolades, they are still children of God who need healing, comforting, and grace. Do preachers and church folk have time to love?

"Can the church say Amen?" Pastor Marlon threw his hands in the air completing the closing prayer.

"Amen!" Church members cried out from the pews.

"I have been thanking the Lord for all of my many blessings." He said looking out into the congregation. "Lord knows I've been truly blessed. Have you all taken the time to just thank him? Have you thanked him for all the many blessing he has bestowed upon you?" Pastor Marlon asked scanning the front row just in time to catch a glimpse of Sister Franklin crossing her legs with a short skirt on.

"Whew!" Pastor Marlon handkerchief in hand, wiped his eyes, cleared his throat while jumping back and almost choked when he noticed that Sister Franklin was not wearing any panties. "Um, yes! I have been thanking the Lord for ALL my many blessings. Have you? I mean we sometimes have a tendency to complain to the Lord and ask him to fix what is wrong, but what I'm asking you is have you thanked him lately for all that he has done right?"

A few members raised their hands and shook their heads. The phrase "Thank you Lord" was heard repeatedly throughout the sanctuary.

"I know I have!" Teresa, who has never missed a single one of his preaching engagements, stated loudly looking Pastor Marlon directly in his eyes.

"Yes, thank you Lord." Pastor Marlon responded grinning at Teresa.

Pastor Marlon looked down to the other end of the front row and jumped when his eyes met a pair of double D breasts escaping the shirt of a beautiful young woman he didn't not recognize. His wife, Shelby looked at him with a raised eyebrow.

Pastor Marlon adjusted his tie. "I especially want to thank my beautiful wife, Shelby, for supporting me all of these years. I would not be standing here if it weren't for the support of my wife. They say behind every great man, there is a great woman. Shelby is a great woman and she has been right beside me every step of the way.

Shelby held her head high with a smile plastered across her face. Teresa's smile had faded by now. A few other women displayed pursed lips and rolled their eyes.

Pastor Marlon sermonically paused for a moment. He had just finished delivering a powerful message at bible study and looked around his church again. He was pleased with what he saw.

"Can you all believe that five years ago we only had four members?" He asked addressing the congregation. He simply posed the rhetorical question out loud. Now we have grown to over fifteen hundred members and over twenty-three ministries.

"Mmmm Hmmm, well." Simultaneously church members shook their heads in agreement.

"Can the church say Amen?"

"Amen!"

"I can't hear you. I said can the church say Amen?"

"Amen!" The congregation responded loudly.

"Now I want to thank all of you for whom without there would be no church. Thank you for being faithful members, paying your tithes and supporting our building fund as we prepare to continue to grow and move on to bigger and better places. I will see you all again on Sunday morning. If anyone needs prayer or counseling with me please see me directly after bible study. Good night."

The congregation dispersed separate ways and Pastor Marlon gathered his bible after shaking a few hands and was greeted by his wife.

"Thank you honey. You did an awesome job tonight, as usual."

"Thank you Shelby. You know I meant every word."

"I know. I will see you at home." Shelby kissed Pastor Marlon on the cheek.

"Okay, I will be right home after everyone has cleared out."

"Do you promise?"

"I promise."

"Okay, in that case I will let the kids stay up and wait for you."

"Okay Shelby, I will try my best to wrap this up tonight."

"Okay honey."

The two went their separate ways. Pastor Marlon was greeted at the door by what he recognized as the Double D's that were sitting on the front row during bible study.

"Hi, Pastor. My name is Silvia."

"Nice to meet you, Silvia. How did you enjoy the service tonight?"

"I thought it was amazing. I was really moved."

"I'm very pleased to hear that. Are you just visiting?"

"Yes, well I'm actually new to the area and looking for a church home and just wanted to meet you. I have heard so many good things about you." Silvia extended her hand.

"Well Sister, let me welcome you. It is a pleasure meeting you. Please do not hesitate to let me know if there is anything I can do for you." Pastor Marlon could not help but direct his eyes toward her breasts.

"Well, I have a lot of turmoil in my personal life and have been asking God to see me through it."

"I'm so sorry to hear that. Do you need anything?"

"Well, I understand you give private counseling. Is that right?" Silvia's look became a bit more seductive.

"Um, yes." Pastor Marlon began to rummage through his pockets and Deacon Brown approached him.

"Pastor, there is some business we need to discuss before you leave tonight."

"Yes, I will be right there." Pastor responded retrieving a clergy card from his pocket. "Sister Silvia, here is my card. Please don't hesitate to call me whenever you are in need of counseling or prayer. If you can't come to me I can come wherever you need me to. I do make house calls too."

Silvia returned a mischievous grin and slowly removed the card from Pastor Marlon's hand. "Thank you Pastor."

Pastor Marlon took out a cloth and wiped the sweat from his forehead before heading toward his study. The church had cleared out and Deacon Brown was standing at the door of the study holding a stack of papers in his hand.

"Come on in Deacon." Both men nicely suited up walked inside the study.

"What's up Deacon?" Pastor sat in the big chair behind his desk. "Let's make this quick. I gotta get home tonight at a decent hour. Shelby has been on me lately for not spending enough time at home with the family. She just does not understand all the responsibilities I have here. It's just one of me to go around."

"What? You not pulling an all nighter tonight Pastor?" They both laughed. "Okay, I will make this brief. First, here are some letters personally addressed to you." Deacon Brown placed a stack of envelopes in all different sizes on the Pastor's desk.

"Thank you, I will look through those tomorrow."

"Next there's the issue with the Robinson's wedding. We have been going back and forth with them on the logistics and we finally set a date that works with your schedule. There are a few more minor issues but we need to know if you are going to agree to conducting their ceremony before we move forward?"

"Was that the couple having trouble making the full payment?"

"Yes, and we said we would get back to them. I didn't know if you would be willing to work with them since they have been faithful members of the church since it's inception."

"Have they paid their tithes on time every month?"

"Well Pastor you asked me that before and I told you that they had not paid when he lost his job and times were hard when the economy went down. However, when he became employed again he reestablished his tithing pattern. It only took him a year and a half to get back on his feet."

"A year and a half! That's a lot of missed tithes."

"Pastor you did say you would consider possibly making a concession for this lovely couple trying to make a new start together."

"I see. Well, I just have too much on my plate. If they can't make the full payment, I can't do it. What's next?" Pastor Marlon was abrupt with his answer.

"Okay, can you meet with the Deacon Board this Sunday before church to discuss your request for another raise?" Deacon Brown had a hint of sarcasm in his voice.

"Now that I can definitely do!" Pastor Marlon rubbed his hands together grinning. "I have been under a lot of stress working so hard with building the new church, preparing these sermons, holding bible study, and leading the counseling sessions."

"I understand that Pastor. I know you have had a lot fall on your shoulders and Deacon Smith said he was more than willing to help you out with some of your private counseling sessions to take some of the load off of you." Deacon Brown explained.

"Uh, well no, no now that won't be necessary."

"Look Pastor, I'm not trying to be funny but it seems like you may have your hands full." Deacon Brown explained in a low tone.

"What do you mean?"

"I mean I see the scenery on that front row. Not just at bible study, but on Sunday's too. Man, I saw the Double D's!" Deacon Brown laughed. "Pastor I don't mean any disrespect, but a man would be crazy not to be tempted, even a little bit. I mean think about it."

Pastor Marlon kept a straight face. "God placed these women, I mean people in my life for me to help them, for me to give them what they need. I will remain faithful and obedient to my ministry."

"And what a great ministry it is!" Deacon Brown chuckled.

Pastor Marlon began to speak looking in the air across the room. "Deacon Brown my wish is that I can do the Lawd's will, so on that great day I can get my crown. So on that great day, the Lawd can say to me, 'Marlon, well done! Well done, good and faithful servant!' I know I ain't perfect. I know this!"

"But the women. I mean, I see how they just throw themselves at you. It's like you're famous or something."

Pastor Marlon continues looking across the room. "Maybe it's a treat from God for being faithful and for working for nearly nothing all those years."

Deacon Brown shrugged his shoulders and replied. "Okay Pastor. You don't have to explain anything to me." Deacon Brown knew that the Pastor really didn't truly believe his last theodicy statement and he was not interested in hearing anymore explanations to justify his behavior. "I just have some papers here for you to sign concerning the new building fund and I will get out of here. Did you want me to wait on you?" Deacon Brown arranged the papers on the desk.

"There you are." Pastor Marlon placed his pen back in his desk drawer after adorning each page with his signature. "Now, you can get out of here. I might as well start working on my sermon for Sunday since I'm here. Shelby will just have to understand."

"Alright Pastor. You have a good night. Don't work too hard."

"Goodnight, Deacon Brown. I won't work any harder than the Lord expects me too." Pastor Marlon responded turning the pages in his bible.

Deacon Brown walked out and closed the door behind him. Moments later there was a knock at the sacristy door. Pastor Marlon didn't expect anyone to disturb him during this private time.

"Deacon Brown is that you? Did you forget something?"

Pastor Marlon got up and walked around his desk and opened the door. Teresa was standing there in a trench coat.

"No, its not Deacon Brown. Can I come in?" Teresa replied in a sexy voice.

Pastor Marlon's heart began to race. "Of course, you can come in." Pastor Marlon looked her up and down as she walked past. His eyes landed on the five-inch red patent leather stiletto heels she was sporting.

"I really enjoyed the service tonight. You really preached the word tonight."

"I'm pleased that you enjoyed tonight's service. Yes … the Lord gave me that word." Pastor Marlon was still checking her out.

"That word had to be for me, cause it felt like you were looking right through me!"

"It means so much to me that you felt as if I were speaking directly to you.

"Ummm Hmmm." Teresa responded flirtatiously.

"I was. I want all of my parishioners to feel special, and loved. Of course, I don't mind giving further explanation of that passage in Matthew." Pastor Marlon slowly walked toward her and put his arms around her waist. They swayed side to side as he caressed her back with his hands.

"Really?"

"You are a special woman and I want to do all that I can to help you grow in the Lord. I want to give you all of my undivided attention. That's what you want isn't it?"

"Of course."

"You want me to lay hands on you again?" Pastor Marlon gently caressed her neck with his lips and pulled her closer.

"Oh please ... Do you mind? I need that! I need some healing, right now! Thank you Jesus!" Teresa closed her eyes enjoying every moment.

"Oh, I don't mind at all baby. After all ... it's my job. It's part of my calling. You want me to take your coat?"

"Sure," Teresa responded and slowly began opening her trench coat.

"Whoa!!" Pastor jumped back in shock. "You're not wearing anything underneath that coat!"

"Well, I enjoyed round one so much before bible study I just thought I would come back for round two. That is if that's okay with you?" Teresa asked dropping her coat to the floor.

"Damn baby!" Pastor Marlon cleared his throat. "I mean, let me know your needs. I am here to serve you." Pastor Marlon put his arms around her body and gently kissed her on the neck.

"Oh, Marlon." Teresa moaned.

"Now you know you're supposed to call me Pastor ... I am still your Pastor." Pastor Marlon explained.

"Okay ... Pastor!" Teresa responded.

"Umm Hmmmm." Marlon forcefully grabbed her, pulling her body close to his.

Ring ...Ring ...Ring

They both jumped when the phone rang. Pastor Marlon looked at Teresa and put one finger to her mouth.

"Hello."

"Oh, hey Shelby. Yeah, I know I said I would be straight home. I, I just let time get away from me. I got immersed in this sermon I'm writing for Sunday." Pastor Marlon turned his back to Teresa.

"You know I love to spend time with you and the kids."

"Shelby, will you just listen."

"Shelby ... okay Shelby. Now will you just listen and stop yelling."

"Look Shelby, don't start this again. I have a job to do. This is what God has called me to do! Now, I will be home as soon as I am finished up here."

"Goodbye." Pastor Marlon paused a minute after hanging up the phone. Then proceeded to walk back over to Teresa placing an arm around her waste. "Now where were we?"

"I was telling you how much I enjoyed the service this evening." Teresa replied. "I especially enjoyed the part where you started hollerin' and sweatin', and pantin', talkin' about sowing seeds." Teresa was breathing real heavy between her words.

"Really?" Pastor Marlon was intrigued and continued caressing her body with both hands.

"Yeah!"

"And why is that?"

"Well, that's what I been doing here. Sowing seeds."

"Is that so?"

"Yes, and in more ways than one."

"Ummm Hmmm!" Pastor Marlon loosened his belt with one hand while gripping her body with the other and kissed on her neck.

"Marlon? I mean Pastor?" Teresa whispered softly in his ear. "When are you leaving Shelby?"

Marlon immediately froze. "Shelby?" He then pulled back away from Teresa.

"Yes, Shelby! Your wife!"

"Whoa! Whoa! Wait! What are you talking about?"

"You know what I'm talking about! You said that God wanted us to be together and that we should leave our spouses so that we could be obedient!"

"What are you talking about Teresa? I never said anything like that! Are you crazy?" Pastor Marlon picked up Teresa's coat and motioned for her to put it back on. He paused to think for a minute and it hit him. He remembered the night he said those things to her just to get her to sleep with him. He just said what he had to, to have his way with her. He shook his head and wondered why he went so far with this one. Then remembered how mesmerized he was by Teresa's body and how smart she is. She paid her tithes, she is in the choir, and never missed an engagement. She even did things that Shelby doesn't believe in doing cause she thinks God frowns on those things. Teresa is a daring risk taker. He continued looking at her in silence. *She deserves so much better. I don't deserve her.*

"Why are you just looking at me?" Teresa grabbed her coat and began putting her arms through the sleeves. "So now I'm crazy? Look Marlon, I know exactly what you said. I've left my husband, broken up my family, and you don't want to keep up your end of the bargain?"

"What, Teresa?"

Teresa was not happy with his response. "What? Oh naw! Hell naw! Negro you gon' keep your word. You ole' lyin' ass preacha!" Teresa came toward him in a threatening manner with one hand raised.

Pastor Marlon grabbed her arm and began to speak calmly, "Wait Teresa! Now come on. Where is all of this coming from? You know I'm married and I have children. If I leave my wife, I lose my church and you know I'm up for bishop ... If I lose my church and lose my wife, I break up a happy home. Do you understand my predicament?"

"Marlon, I'm married with children too! What's that supposed to mean?"

"It's Pastor! And keep your voice down!" Marlon whispered with a finger to his lip.

"Negro, please! Tonight it's Marlon and I'll get loud if I want to!" Teresa yelled waving both hands in the air.

Pastor Marlon calmly replied, "What do you want Teresa?"

"Marlon you know what I want." Teresa looked Pastor Marlon directly in the eyes.

"I thought I did when you walked in here wearing nothing under that coat and I was ready to give you whatever you wanted. Now, I don't know what you expect from me." Pastor Marlon held his head down.

Teresa walked up to Pastor Marlon and put one hand under his chin gently raising his head. Their eyes met and she spoke sternly. "Marlon you know what I want. And if you don't hold up to your end of the bargain, you can kiss your church, your reputation, and your family goodbye!"

The Black Man-O-logues

Jacquay Waller

Custody

When it comes to issues of parental custody and children, one can almost always assume the children will end up with the mother. Why is that? Is it because women are better parents? Is it because men can't handle the pressure? Is it that they can't do it; that they don't want to do it? How can fathers persuade society to recognize that they fill a pertinent role in the lives of children? How can society persuade fathers to step up in order to let go of their boyhood and grab on to their manhood?

The Black Man-O-logues

Honk, Honk!

Brian sat in his dusty, black four-door Honda Accord stuck in traffic.

Great! Just what I need. I don't even want to hear her mouth when I get there late the pick up the kids. The thought, which led Brian to relive what he felt like during the worst moment in his life so far. He thought about the custody case between him and his long-term girlfriend Sherry. He still could not believe they awarded her primary custody of their three children. In court, she and her attorney were able to paint a picture of him that was just not true. The words of her attorney still haunt him.

"Brian has shown how irresponsible he is. Look at his criminal history, look at his terrible financial decisions causing him to not only file bankruptcy but to foreclose on a home too. A man like that cannot be trusted to raise these children!..."

Brian crept along with the slow traffic shaking his head. He felt defeated and wondered if there was anything he could do. The thought of only seeing his kids every other weekend from now on was killing him. He grabbed his cell phone and dialed his lawyer.

"Hello. Yes, is Burney available?"

"Yes, I'll hold." Brian gripped the steering wheel tighter.

"Burney, you have to tell me if there is anything I can do about this custody situation? I mean this is hell for me. I am used to seeing my kids on a daily basis."

"What do you mean this can go on for months?" Brian yelled in the phone.

"I know, I know. I just don't have that kind of money Burney."

"I see. So do you think I have a good chance at getting custody?" Brian lowered his tone and listened to the options Burney laid out over the phone.

"I understand. Sure Burney, I'll settle for another arrangement that allows me to see them more often. This every other weekend shit just ain't gonna cut it."

"I know you understand my pain. How can any father not? I am one of the good ones. I'm the Dad that's trying to raise his kids and spend time with them.

I mean those are my babies. I would do anything for them." Brian was comforted by Burney's words.

"I know you understand."

"It's just that I was looking forward to teaching my sons how to be polite; how to be gentlemen; how to be productive citizens. I want to teach them how to be much better than I was, and than I am. I'm supposed to teach them the proper way to treat women and to expose them to all kinds of types of music ... besides Hip Hop. You know I won't even let my kids listen to Hip Hop if it's too vulgar or doesn't paint the right picture. They're going to have enough problems just being Black in America. I want to make sure my daughter loves herself and knows that she is loved. I want her to know she doesn't have to be defined by music, videos, and TV. I don't want my daughter out here getting lipo-suction and implants because she didn't have her Daddy around to tell her how beautiful she is."

"I'm sorry Burney, I know I'm rambling. I won't hold you. It's just that this shit is eating me up day and night."

"Alright, I'll hang in there. Just know you'll be hearing from me again when I can't take no more of this shit."

"Thanks Burney, I'm glad I have a friend like you. I appreciate you listening to my problems and handling my case so well. And of course not charging me an arm and a leg for this!"

"Talk to you later." Brian ended the call.

Brian finally got past the car wreck that caused all of the traffic. He looked forward to seeing his children and at the same time dreaded seeing his ex-girlfriend, Sherry.

When he pulled up Sherry was standing at the door.

Aw hell… Here we go… Brian slowly got out of his car and closed the door taking his time walking up to the front door.

"You told me you would be here an hour ago!" Sherry yelled.

"Look Sherry-". Brian pleaded.

"Don't look Sherry me!"

"Why you got to yell? Lower your voice, damn! You ain't in that much of a hurry. You still got house shoes on!"

"Whatever!"

"Ok, Sherry will you please step out here? I don't want the kids to hear us." Brian painfully requested.

Sherry rolled her eyes and folded her arms at the same time. She closed the door and walked closer to where Brian was standing.

"Anyway, what took you so long? I got some place to go." Sherry was still furious, but spoke in a lower tone.

"I got here as soon as I could Sherry. I got off late to begin with and there was a wreck on the expressway." Brian explained.

"Unnh, huh. I bet! I see ain't nothing changed." Sherry rolled her eyes.

"What are you talking about Sherry? Ain't nothing changed! What needed to change!" Brian raised his voice.

"Are you serious? Why do you think we're not together anymore? You only wanted to do things that benefited you. If you had nothing to gain you didn't want anything to do with it. Don't you see what's wrong with that?" Sherry huffed.

"Is that the reason you wanted to see other people?" Brian asked.

"If I remember correctly, you suggested that we see other people. You don't remember?" Sherry asked. "Are you ok?"

"Yeah I'm fine. Look Sherry, I been wanting to talk to you."

"Talk to me about what? I got somewhere to be!" Sherry snapped.

"I just don't see how you sat there and let them paint that picture of me in court. You know I am a good father. I've always spent more time with them than you!"

"Not the court shit again. Brian get over it. The courts agree with me. The kids should be with their mother." Sherry smirked.

"Man, fuck the courts! I'm not talking about the courts. I'm talking about me and you and our kids." Brian threw both hands up and shot her a deadly look.

"Brian, what is that you want?" Sherry put her hands on her hips.

"Sherry you know you didn't have to let it get so ugly is all I'm saying. I mean who took them to school. Me!" Brian pointed at his own chest with each statement. "Who picked them up from school? Me! I was the one who read to them before they went to bed. Who did the school call if one of the kids got in trouble? It certainly wasn't you!" Brian wiped the sweat from his forehead.

Sherry opened her mouth to speak.

"Wait, I'm not finished!" Brian held his hand up and interjected before she could begin. "I would go on the field trips. I would volunteer at the school. I even went to the PTA meetings. How the hell you gone say I'm an unfit father?" Brian pointed at himself with every example he threw out.

"And!! What's your point Brian? I don't know why you telling me all this. I don't have time for this." Sherry shook her head.

"Sherry you may not have time for this but I love my kids and my kids love me. I am one of the few black men trying to be in their kids' life more and you are taking that away from me. Ya'll trying to make me out to be a statistic. One of those father's not around for their kids contributing to communities being in such bad shape due to the lack of black male visibility, responsibility, and availability. Sherry I am visible, responsible and I'm damn sho' available." Brian pounded himself on the chest.

Sherry began to clap. "Bravo! Bravo!" She responded condescendingly. "Thanks for the speech Brian but it's too late for all that. I'm moving on with my life and like I told you when you got here, I have to go. Now, it's time for you to get the kids and go too."

Brian shook his head. He wasn't sure what he expected her to say, but he was unwilling to give up. "Wait Sherry!"

"Brian, what do you want?" Sherry huffed.

"I just think this has gone too far. I was just hoping we could work out our differences and become a family again. You know we made a great couple. We were beautiful together. Think about our kids. They would be happy again. You know a weekend is not enough time to raise my kids."

"Brian, I'm not going to keep going back and forth with you about the same thing."

"You say that like it's not important." Brian felt desperate. "Sherry can we just talk about this, please. Isn't our family worth a few minutes of your time?"

"Brian, there is nothing for us to talk about. The answer is No! You know I'm engaged, right? Keith proposed to me last week."

Brian lowered his head. "You're joking right?"

Sherry leaned in and flashed her ring. "You didn't notice the rock?"

Brian took a quick glance. "Naw, I didn't know ya'll were that serious. I really didn't think you liked him like that. He's not even your type. Plus, the kids said he didn't even want kids." Brian displayed a confused look.

"What?" Sherry looked shocked.

"Well, does he even want kids? That's an important question to ask when you got three of them."

"I- I mean he didn't at first, but he's coming around. Anyway that's not any of your business." Sherry stuttered.

"Anything involving my kids is my business. Shit, I don't' want my kids callin' some other nigga' Daddy! I'm they Daddy! You better believe it will be my business if he mistreats any one of them in the slightest way."

"Brian, stop wasting my time. Now I'm about to go." Sherry turned to walk back toward the house. Brian grabbed her arm. Sherry jerked away.

"Now, you going too far. You better keep your damn hands off of me! I will have the police over to lock you up in a heartbeat if you lay your hands on me again." Sherry yelled.

Brian threw his hands up. "Sherry, you know I have never tried to physically hurt you. Why are you being so goddamned dramatic?"

Sherry stood fuming with both hands on her hips.

"Oh, I get it. That's what you want, ain't it? You already humiliated me in court. You got me on this fucked up schedule and I can't even see my kids when I want. Now you want me in jail! After all I've done. Don't you think ever think about how it used to be between us Sherry?" Brian pleaded.

"Brian we are friends. Friends without benefits. Please be sure to drop the kids off by 8:00pm. They have to be in the bed by 9:00pm, so they can be rested for school just like the court order says." Sherry turned away was done having the conversation.

Brian was burning up inside, but his resolve melted and he swallowed his pride while thinking about the big picture… his family. "I'll see what I can do. One more question though."

Sherry turned her attention back to Brian.

"So, all the work I did at home, with the kids, in the yard, all the overtime on the job … it didn't count for nothin? I did it all for you. For us! I did it for our family. I thought we would grow old together and travel the world." Brian made his final plea.

"As far as I'm concerned Brian, you did it all for you. Yeah we saw some benefits, but that's the past now." Sherry walked to the door to open it. "Enough of this! You got to go! Keith will be back shortly." Sherry open the door and yelled upstairs. "Kids! Your Daddy's ready! Grabs your bags and come on!"

"But, but, Sherry …" Brian shook his head in disgust feeling defeated.

"But, buh, bye, bye Brian!" Sherry stepped back inside the door and opened it up.

"Come on guys. Your Daddy is waiting for you. Let's go!" Sherry looked back at Brian and rolled her eyes.

"Sherry, I'm not going to just let you remove my kids from my life only letting me see them when your schedule allows. Just know that! I love and care about my kids far to much not to do anything about it. If it's a court order you want to follow, then we will just have to see about getting that changed. I refuse to be a weekend father! Raising my kids is a twelve month, 365 day, 24 hour job!"

The kids walked outside carrying their back packs. "What's up Dad?"

"Come on guys let's go enjoy our weekend." Brian walked put his arms around his kids and walked them to the car. "I love you guys!"

"We love you too Dad!" The kids smiled heading to the car.

Brian got in the car and picked up his cell phone and dialed.

"Yes, is Burney available."

Jacquay Waller

C
U
S
T
O
D
Y

"Okay yes. I'll hold."

The Black Man-O-logues

Jacquay Waller

Our Wisdom

Why do many fear growing older? The word is out ... people are living longer and better. Sixty is the new fifty, fifty is the new forty, forty is the new thirty, thirty is the new twenty, and I guess that would make twenty the new, ten? When will people reach out to our elderly? There is so much knowledge and wisdom sitting there waiting to be shared. There are stories there that will never be written down which hold the potential to change lives and attitudes. What can be done about this gap of age and culture? Is it possible that we could share similar experiences?

"Man, that shit don't make no sense. I done had every pair of Jordans ever made! That, my nigga, makes me the man." The first boy said dribbling the ball then passing it.

"So! That shit don't make you the man." The second boy retorted.

"Well, I think it does. I got my shoes by any means necessary. Plus, me and my man Jordan share the same first name."

"Nobody cares Mike, man, I ain't tryin' to beat no nigga ass for no Jay's!" The second boy said shooting and missing. "My seventeen years of life has taught me a thing or two."

"Shit, a nigga gotta do what a nigga gotta do!" Mike got the rebound and jumped up dunking the ball. He came down halting the game to wipe off his shoes. "Seventeen! Chris, you only one year older than me."

Gramps sat in the park enjoying the weather as he did every Sunday afternoon, listening to the young boys talk and watching them play basketball. He just shook his head this day listening to them talk about what makes them 'the man'.

"Um, excuse me." Gramps said in an attempt to get their attention.

The boys kept talking as if they did not hear a word.

Gramps decided to get a little louder. He beat his cane on the bench he was sitting on and yelled. "Hey! Youngblood! Let me talk with ya."

Everyone stopped and looked at the old man sitting on the bench.

"Hey Pops! You talkin' to us?" Mike responded.

"Yes, and I would appreciate it if you addressed me as sir. Don't you have any respect for your elders? Nigga this and nigga that." Gramps responded directly.

"Man forget that old man." Mike said dribbling the ball again.

"Sorry about that sir." Chris said feeling a little sorry for the old man.

"Thank you, at least one of you got a little respect. Now watch the language!. When you use a lot of curse words, it means you don't know how to express yourself."

"What that old man talkin' bout?" Mike asked.

"Come over here and I'll tell you what I'm talkin' bout." Gramps imitated him by talking with a little slang. "I might even teach you a thing or two."

Mike waved him off. "That old man talkin' crazy. He can't teach me nothin' I don't already know."

Chris turned to the first boy and said, "Come on man, let's just see what the old man has to say."

Mike dribbled the ball and laughed. "Aight. This might just be fun."

Both boys walked over to the bench where the old man was sitting.

"Okay old man. What you think you can teach us some of that old school shit?"

"See, that's part of the problem. Ya'll ain't got no respect for your elders or anyone in authority. I bet you been locked up before." Gramps pointed to Mike.

"Yeah, I been locked up. I did my time." Mike laughed.

"You think that's something to be proud of. I won't even ask what you got locked up for. Probably fighting or stealing."

"Hey, how did you know?" Mike laughed and punched the Chris in the arm. "Old man, I bet you never been to jail."

"Oh, I been to jail. Just not the way you little negroes are now going to jail."

"What's that supposed to mean? I ain't bout to let nobody disrespect me."

"I went to jail helping my people. Ya'll go to jail for hurting my people. Actually our people. It's a big difference." Gramps explained.

"You right, I'm gone hurt somebody 'fore I let them hurt me. What you get locked up for anyway old man, jaywalking?" Chris chuckled and shot Mike a look for approval.

"I got locked up for boycotting, protesting, standing up for rights. The same rights you take for granted now. What's your names?"

They both grew silent. Mike dribbled the ball back and forth between his legs.

Chris's smile faded and he looked at Mike, then back at Gramps. "I'm Chris and this is my cousin Mike."

"So where are your daddies?"

"Why you askin' bout our Daddies?" Mike got defensive.

"Cause he probably ain't around, I suspect."

"Watch it old man. That's personal." Mike snapped back.

"Just what I thought. Daddies ain't nowhere around, in the streetz, locked up, slanging rocks, trying to be rappers, chasing that bling, bling. See in my day, Daddies wanted to be around to ensure their boys became men. They made sure dem boys had something to do to keep them out of trouble. Girls too! Now, I ain't sayin' we were always angels and didn't have problems in my day. After all, we had to deal with being called nigga, coon, running from lynch mobs, sneaking through back doors, fighting back against those who were suppose to protect and serve, battling crazy dogs and mean water."

Both boys stared at Gramps hanging on to every word.

"Nowadays, our young black folk call each other nigga and think its cute. They crazy as hell!" Gramps threw his hands up in the air.

"Man, callin' my boy nigga ain't nothin' like it was in yo day. My niggas know its cool. When we say it, it don't mean the same as when the white people said it. So, it's cool."

"But it ain't cool. How you gone decide the same word can have a different meaning just because the person saying it is black and not white. That don't even make no sense." Gramps shook his head.

"Pops, you wouldn't understand. You might know a lot about the old days but you don't know shit about what's going on today."

"That's what you think. I know all about that Hippity Hoppity stuff."

Both boys laugh this time.

"What is that mess anyway? Most of the stuff I hear has either bitch this or hoe dat. And if it's on the radio it's bleep this or bleep that. A lot of times they don't even bleep it."

"Aw Pops, you worried about the wrong things. You might want to stick to your oldies but goodies station." The boys slapped hands and laughed.

"My grandson keeps me up to date with some of the latest music. He teaches me some of the latest dances too."

"Pops, what dances you think you know about?" Mike inquired doubtfully.

Gramps started leaning to the side and bouncing to the music in his head, "Oh, I know how to lean wit it and rock wit it. I know about the White T's and the Dougy!" Gramps brushed his hand over his head demonstrating his rendition of the Dougy.

OUR WISDOM

The boys jumped up laughing. "Alright Pops! You might just know a little something for your age."

"You shouldn't laugh at an old man. Let me tell you something. I talk to my grandson about that music. So he can make some good choices and not be influenced by what the music means and what it's saying."

"What you mean Pops? It's just music! Old people always trying to spoil our fun. We just like the beats and we just be dancing. What's the big deal?"

"Listen Boy! ... I know it sounds good and I know you're just dancing ... but what is the music saying? Are you really listening?"

"Yeah, we hear the words and it's not a big deal. What's your point Pops?" Chris shrugged.

"Would you want anybody to talk to your Mama or your sister or even your grandmother the way they do in those songs?"

"No!"

"Would you talk to your Mama the way they do in those songs?"

"Hell no! My Mama would whoop my ass!"

"That's my point! Why would you talk to any woman that way? You see in my day- ..."

"Here we go!" Mike rolled his eyes cutting the old man off.

"That's your problem right there. You ain't got no respect! You see more of you young black folks need to talk to us old folk. We ain't goin' sugar coat nothing! We keeps it real witcha. Now as I was saying ... back in my day, a lot of folks called the blues and dem slow songs devil music, but we still listened. But you see, we weren't all out robbing and killing one another. We didn't run off and leave our wife and kids alone."

"What you talkin' bout Pops? I ain't got no wife." Chris was amused at his comment.

"Exactly ... Back then, if you got a girl pregnant, you married her. You made it work! You made sure you took care of your responsibilities. We weren't trying to be locked up for killing, robbing, gang bangin' or drugs. We really cared about our people." Gramps was passionate.

"All black men ain't like that old man. When I have kids, I'm gone be there and take care of them. I ain't gone be like my Daddy!" The first boy gave a serious look.

"Son, I love all black men but I'm certainly not proud of all black men. I thought the number of black men going to college was on the rise but now its falling again. Even, worse, now there are more young black folks dropping out of high school. The number of black men in prison continues to rise. What's going on? Why won't black men do better?"

"Pops, I know you mean well, but why you coming down on black men so hard? What about the women?" Chris asked.

"I know black women can do better too. Like by not making excuses for no good men."

"What's that supposed to mean? They should put down black men too?" Mike questioned.

"They ain't got to put 'em down ... that's not what I'm saying. But it is a way to support a man and help him along without being a crutch for him. They don't need to let them boys use 'em ... only to make a baby, disappear ... and start all over again. These women should think more highly of themselves."

"Alright Dr. Phil! I have gotten all the life lessons I can stand today. I'm 'bout to go play some ball." Mike commented bouncing his ball on the ground.

"You know young man, there was a time when we really cared about our people. We loved you! We loved you before you even came along."

"There were a lot of folks in my generation who died 'cause they wanted a better life for their kids, grandkids, great-grandkids, and all the generations that followed. I wouldn't tell you this if I didn't love you."

Both boys stood still looking dumbfounded. "But you don't even know us. Why would you care?"

"Young man, it is my responsibility while I am here on this earth to do my part. That's what I'm trying to do. Young brothers don't even know how to court a girl. They don't know how to surprise her, open doors for her, and to make her feel special."

"All this talk about love, where's your wife Pops?" Chris asked.

Gramps looked up to the sky and smiled. "Well, I was married for fifty-three years before my wife got called home. She was the only woman besides my mother and sisters that I ever loved. And I tell you, there was no one, and there never will be anyone, I'll love like I loved Cecilia." Gramps shook his head and the boys listened intently. "She was beautiful, and I told her that all the time. We would spend a lot of time together just holding one another and dreaming. Anything she wanted to do, I would support her on it. Even if I didn't agree, I would voice it, but I would support her if that was what she wanted. And she would do the same for me. If it felt like the whole world was against me, I knew I always had someone on my side, Cecilia. Oh, I can see her smile now. She always had the most beautiful teeth. Um ... and boy ... she could shole ... uh ... never mind."

They all laughed.

"Pops gettin' freaky!" Mike joked.

Gramps chuckled. "I just miss her so much. "

A couple passing by hand in hand had stopped walking and stood mesmerized by Gramps talking about his wife.

"I always admired her for many things, but one thing in particular was how she would let me be a man. You know brothers be wanting to lead some things and protect their family, you know, make everybody safe. We just want to provide for our family and make sure folks are happy. At least that's how I was. But looking back, Cecelia was really leading because she was my conscience. Everything I wanted was for us. It was like our souls were joined. I couldn't imagine living life without ever meeting her. It wasn't always easy. We didn't always see eye to eye. You see the difference between us and a lot of folks was that we could agree to disagree. We had respect for each other. We understood that a marriage, a relationship, takes work. It took work! For us, it took 53 years worth of work.

OUR WISDOM

That's what its about. That's all I'm trying to tell you brothas. Long lasting, unforgettable, unconditional love. The love I have for my Cecelia, my kids and grandkids. The love I have for my people. Young brothers ... this is the love I have for you. I want ya'll to step up and become the men I know you can become. You hear?"

"Yeah, we hear you Pops. We get it. It's on us now. It's on us." Chris responded.

The boys looked at each other and began to walk away bouncing their basketball. Mike turned back to the old man. "Thanks Sir. Thanks ..."

The Black Man-O-logues

Jacquay Waller

True Love

Does true love really exist? Does true black love really exist? What does it look like? Everybody has vision of what true love is. It is already fixated in an individual's mind, it's taste, it's smell, it's build. Where is it? Does monogamous love work?

"Man, how did you know Rita was the one?" Phil asked trying to get some advice about his own relationship. "I mean how did you know you wanted to marry her?"

George held the phone to his ear as he straightened up the living room. "Shoot, I didn't think we needed to get married, but after thinking about it, where was I going? The sex was good, real good. We paying the bills ... on time ... I like her folks and they seem to like me. My folks are crazy about her and she's crazy about them. We have been blessed. Our life is good. Our kids are happy ... I figured we may as well take the last step."

"You make it sound so simple." Phil was frustrated.

"Look man, its as simple as you make it. Rita even got me going to church. I wasn't feeling church at first. I thought all those preachers were pimps who had the women wrapped around their fingers. And I still think a lot of 'em are, but not all. Kudos to my wife of course. Our pastor is cool. He can break off some

Word! And he ain't too good to shake your hand after service neither!" George laughed.

"George man, I just don't want to do anything over here and have regrets. Didn't you feel the same way about that girl before Rita?"

"Yeah, I thought she was the one. I mean she looked good. She was good in bed. She was good with my kids, my folks liked her, but we argued a lot. And she was a terrible cook. Man, I tried eating the food because she worked so hard to prepare it. But it seemed like I spent more time in the bathroom than I did at the dinner table. She tried, but it just wasn't meant for us. We dated on and off for a year, but it just didn't feel right. We moved in together after two months to see if we could take it further. Man, that was a bad idea!" George laughed.

"I think it's a good idea. I was thinking of asking Justine to move in just to test it out myself. What do you think?" Phil asked sounding unsure of himself.

"I can't tell you what to do but I learned really quick that my last girl and I were great lovers but terrible roommates. I will tell you, I got mad respect for Rita though. I asked her to move in with me after three months, just to test her. She said 'No'."

"Why? I thought that's what all women wanted." Phil replied.

"Yeah, me too. I tried to convince her that it would free up more money for us to travel and go out to concerts and wine tastings and thangs like that. Man, she was not having it. She said we should wait until we are married to move in together. She said that way we will have something to look forward to. I agreed but I was just hoping to see how we interacted first to see if I even wanted to take it there. It never happened."

"Did that make it harder for you to decide if she was the one?" Phil inquired.

"Naw, she even made me wait about eight months before I even got the draws. I liked that! It was a chase. It was challenging. I think she had seen her friends hurt or had been hurt and didn't want to go there again. She just thought better of herself. She

TRUE LOVE

knew she deserved better. She deserved the best. And that is what I strive to give her. Man, she will be home in a minute and I want to have this house straight for her."

"Damn, she got you like that?" Phil laughed.

"Don't hate now. I'll tell you this, if I have to work until I'm in my grave to give her the world, I will. Cause I know she would do the same for me. I thank God for sending me a partner, a friend, a lover, a teacher, a student, a roadie, a wife. Now let me go so I can get ready for my wife to get home."

"Alright man, I just need to figure this shit out." Phil sounded down.

"I'll holla at you tomorrow at work."

They both hung up the phone just as the door was opening.

"Hey baby." Rita walks in and greets George with a kiss.

"What's up gorgeous? How are you?" George held her tight around her waist.

"I'm fine …"

"Yes ... yes ... you are." George looked Rita up and down. "How was your day?"

"Oh .. it was okay. I'm just glad to be home. How was your day?"

"You know, the usual. It's time to switch jobs or something. I hate going to that place everyday." George walked across the room.

Rita narrowed her eyes and put her hands on her hips looking directly at George. "You're not about to quit are you?"

George turned to come back with his hands out. "Awe baby! Now come on. Let's not do this."

"Do what?" Rita asked pushing his hands away. "I'm just asking are you about to quit? I need to know cause we been making ends meet and we can't make it on one paycheck." Rita rolled her eyes again feeling resentment stemming from the arguments in the past about the same thing.

"No baby. Come on." George tried putting his arms around Rita and was rejected. "I'm not about to quit my job. Well, not until I get another one." He reassured her. "Now come here with your sexy self."

Rita softened and allowed him to hug her. "Thanks sexy. I knew you wouldn't. I just thought I'd ask, just in case you were crackin' up or somethin'."

"Naw I'm straight. I can't leave my baby hangin like that, can I?" George smirked pulling Rita's body closer to his.

"No, you can't!" Rita snapped.

The two stood in the living room sharing an embrace.

"I was just talking to Phil before you got here. He is trying to figure out if Justine in the one."

"What? Phil thinking about marriage. I gotta see this!" Rita laughed. "Now come on and I'll make dinner for us. I'm getting hungry."

"I'm just glad I don't have to worry about that. You know you will always be the one for me right?"

"Yes baby. I know." Rita replied.

"Wait ... Do I tell you I love you enough? I mean do you need to hear it more?" George looked Rita directly in the eyes. "Can you see how much I love you?"

A smile crept across Rita's face. "I never doubted your love for me. I feel very loved in this home. You show me how much you love me with your words ... your actions ... your hands ... your kisses ... and your tongue." Rita giggled.

George blushed. "Really? Well, you know you do the same for me. I sometimes sit up and think about just how blessed I am to have you in my life. I look forward to growing older and wiser with you Baby."

"George, you gon' make me drop everything right now ... but I don't know...do you want dessert before dinner?" Rita leaned in and kissed him on the neck.

"Oooooh! What about before and after?"

Rita let go and began unbuttoning her shirt giving a sexy grin. "I'm glad you asked." She began walking toward the bedroom.

"What? Right now! Hell Yeah!" George loosened his belt and began to remove his shirt. "Here

I come!" George runs after her, tripping over his pants and unable to contain his excitement.

The Black Man-O-logues

Jacquay Waller

Afterword

You've just been entertained by a book that is laced with deplorable language and appalling situations. But you can't deny that the material presented is true. The situations may not be your situations but may be the reality of someone you know and love. "The Black Man-O-logues" are not meant to be your guiding compass when addressing the issues it presents. I am not dictating "what" or "how" you should to address the problems. However, I do suggest that you do something. In fact, I'm imploring that you do at least three things. The first is to be sure to share these stories with someone else. You will be surprised by the discussions that occur. Secondly, be sure to come out to see "The Black Man-O-logues" the stage play when it comes to your city. There is nothing like seeing these characters in real time. This stage play is an interactive experience that allows the audience to dialogue with the cast.

    And finally, you know I'm a preacher. I want to offer you a prayer for Salvation. I'm not forcing my beliefs upon you. It's just an added bonus! If you are interested in learning how you can be saved, how you can be forgiven of your sins and receive eternal life, go to the next page. Read the listed texts and the prayer of Salvation.

John 3:16

16 For God so loved the world that he gave his one and only Son, that whoever believes in him shall not perish but have eternal life.

In this passage of Scripture we discover that God loved us so much that He sent His only begotten Son Jesus Christ to Earth to die for our sins. So can you imagine this: someone you didn't even know, laid down His life for you?

Romans 10: 9-13

9 If you declare with your mouth, "Jesus is Lord," and believe in your heart that God raised him from the dead, you will be saved. 10 For it is with your heart that you believe and are justified, and it is with your mouth that you profess your faith and are saved. 11 As Scripture says, "Anyone who believes in him will never

be put to shame."[e] 12 For there is no difference between Jew and Gentile — the same Lord is Lord of all and richly blesses all who call on him, 13 for, "Everyone who calls on the name of the Lord will be saved."[f]
In this passage we discover that if we confess with our mouth that Jesus is Lord and believe in our heart that God raised him from the dead that we are Saved.

You don't have to wait until you get your life together before you give your life to the Lord. If you could have done it by yourself, you would have already done it. The Lord knows you're not perfect and he's doesn't expect you to be. Let Him help you. Now understand, just because you're saved, doesn't mean you won't have any problems. For we've learned that God allows the rain to fall on the just and the unjust (Matt. 5:44-45). But know this: you will always have someone who has your back and who has your best interests at heart. If you're interested, pray this prayer:

"Lord God, thank you for my life. I know I am a sinner and I've fallen short of the glory of God. I ask that you

would come into my life and save me. I believe Jesus Christ is Your Son. I believe that you sent Him to Earth to die for my sins. I believe that you raised Him from the dead. I repent of my sins. Please remove anything from me that is unlike you. I love you Lord. Thank You for Saving me!"

AFTERWORD

Congratulations! You're saved!

Your next step should be to find a Church home where you can grow and be nurtured.

Acknowledgements

To live and breathe in this life means to be dependent on others. No one walks alone on this journey called life. It is almost impossible to be successful alone. We need each other. And of course, I'm no different. There are several people to whom I would like to express the utmost gratitude. For without you, this book would not have been possible.

I want to thank God for giving me this vision and incredible gift. I'm still discovering new things and don't always grasp this gift that you've given me but I'm eternally grateful and I thank you for promising to never leave me or forsake me.

I want to thank my wife and my children for their love, support, and patience through the matriculation of the Man-O-logues. I love you and you're always appreciated. You keep me motivated. I also want to thank my wife for also being an influential editor.

I want to thank my parents, Roland and Dorothy, for always doing their best to expose me to new things and pushing me to reach my fullest potential.

To my father-in-law, Carl, my mother-in-law, Georgetta, and my sister in-law Kim, thank you for your love, support, encouragement, and interest in my pursuit of my passion.

ACKNOWLEDGEMENTS

To my siblings, LeAnn, Jan, and Dale, and to the rest of my family, thank you for your love and for being you.

Thank you Tracy for your help on this project and your excitement along the way.

I want to thank one of my mentors and professors, Dr. Alton Pollard. Thank you for always challenging me and encouraging me to think deeply. Your mentorship, encouragement, and personal example has changed me forever.

Thank you Daniel Blanks for being a mentor and friend. You've led by example for years and you continue to help me see the potential in what I do and you're always pressing me to grow. Thank you for leading by walking and not talking.

I want to thank all of my actors who have helped Black Man-O-logues successful. Thank you for talent, commitment, and for being apart of this journey: Rhonda, Tia, Seven-Two, Latoya, Sheffron, Kym, Sam, Bernadette, Autumn, Stephen, Jonathan, Chris, J'Zhanel, DuJuan, Monica, Senay, Latonya, Demario, Reisha, Cassie, Malcolm, P-Funk, Worm, Jacy, Nikki, James, Ali, Simone, and possibly others – please forgive me if I left you out.

I would be remiss not to thank all of my patrons, supporters, and fans. Without you, there would be no

ACKNOWLEDGEMENTS

Black Man-O-logues, DreamCatcher Productions, or DreamCatcher Collective. You continue to inspire me.

To my brother from another mother, Dr. Gregory Shaw, thank you brother for always being there. I don't know where I would be without your encouragement and support, brother. Your calls of encouragement, support, and foolishness are priceless. Thank you for being you. Don't ever change. Thanks for providing a shoulder to lean on.

About the Author

Jacquay Waller, a native of Memphis, Tennessee, has always been destined to be a man of many talents. Jacquay's training in classical music began at a young age and his acting career began as an adolescent. These talents awarded him vocal and academic scholarships to Tennessee State University (TSU), where he earned his Bachelor's Degree in Computer Science.

Upon leaving TSU, Jacquay took his first job in corporate America as rocket scientist for Raytheon Missile Company in Tucson, AZ. Although successful there, he knew that his calling into the ministry could not be ignored and Jacquay enrolled in Candler School of Theology at Emory University. His love for the arts was re-awakened while attending Emory. In his last year of seminary, Jacquay produced and directed the show "Coming From Where I'm From." This directorial debut was the catalyst for launching DreamCatcher Productions in Atlanta, Georgia.

Jacquay re-entered the corporate world not long after obtaining his Master's of Divinity (M.Div.) from Emory University. He even earned his Masters of Business Administration (MBA) from Troy University and his Project Management Professional (PMP) certification. Many would be satisfied with the accolades of the business world and opportunities for advancement found there. However, Jacquay knew he still had to nurture his artistic talents and spiritual goals. He

ABOUT THE AUTHOR

became an accomplished member of AmeriColor Opera Alliance. Some of his performances with them include, "Madame C.J. Walker," "Porgy and Bess," "King Solomon" and the play "Unspoken". He is also the recipient of James A. Hyter award.

While honing his skills through avenues such as opera, local film, and stage performances, Jacquay continued to build DreamCatcher Productions. The company serves a conduit for developing and producing fresh content for the stage and screen. Jacquay serves as actor, writer, director and producer for DreamCatcher Productions. He is the creative genius behind the "Black Man-O-logues" series of stage plays. Other titles from DreamCatcher include, "Black Knight", "The E.N.D.", "Fading Flowers", "Squeeze Pleeze", "Unhappily EverAfter", "The Wishlist", "Race Me", "Bullied", "Traffik", "Suspended", and "Choices."

Jacquay continues to reside in Atlanta, GA with his wife Courtney and their daughter and son. At times, he is a voice for local charitable organizations. He also finds time to lead roundtable discussions on current topics and issues. Jacquay spreads his message of God's love and endurance on stage and from the pulpit.

www.ingramcontent.com/pod-product-compliance
Lightning Source LLC
Chambersburg PA
CBHW051435290426
44109CB00016B/1567